People Are Saying . . .

Karen Clark has done it again! Her new book is a must have for new & seasoned direct selling leaders. The practical advice and step-by-step instructions make this a must have resource for any current or aspiring leader developing their team and business. I think everyone needs to read and reread her section on social media platforms and the questions she provides for online events. I personally want to thank Karen for her work in raising the bar, making our industry more professional and more thoughtful as we move forward. I cannot wait for the next book. (There will be a "next book" — right?) Don't wait. Buy the book now!

DeVerne Augustus, Spokane WA
MONAT Independent Founder & Market Mentor
facebook.com/loveyourhairagainwithdeverne

I absolutely LOVED Karen's new addition to the Social Media for Direct Selling *family! Every kind of leader will be able to take something from this book, whether you've yet to recruit or you're a veteran in the industry! I know I'll be able to suggest this book to everyone on my team regardless of where they are on the commission plan.*

Laura Marshall, Derbyshire England
Independent Younique Presenter
lovelifelashes.co.uk

In addition to working in direct sales for over twelve years, I am also a client retention specialist. Though this book was written "with the independent direct selling leader in mind," I wouldn't hesitate to recommend it to the small business owners I work with. It is well-written, easy to read, and chock full of resources and strategies that can be immediately implemented. It has turned into a resource guide for me. I will be recommending it to my team members as well as my clients. I have already marked up my copy and will be referring back to it repeatedly.

Lucy Kelleher, San Diego CA
Close to My Heart Independent Consultant/
Client Retention Strategist
facebook.com/lucyk.ctmh
facebook.com/keepthemloyal

Karen Clark's two books together are an indispensable Bible on social media. However, this new book, Social Media for Direct Selling Leaders, *takes her first book to a new level. Karen Clark delivers checklists within each topic that help teach you the exact steps to set up and grow your business using social media. She also explains in easy to understand terms how to manage groups, hold team meetings worldwide, and use advanced techniques on many different platforms. I can't wait to go through each section and make sure that my own social media is performing at the highest level possible!*

Gwen Wolken, Northbrook IL
Direct Sales Coach, Trainer, and Speaker
facebook.com/gwenwolken

Karen effortlessly guides leaders through the major social media platforms and decodes the how, when, where, and why! I couldn't be more excited and confident to use social media to grow and manage my business and team! Thank you Karen!

Alice Andreat, Winter Haven FL
Usborne Books & More Independent Consultant
facebook.com/booklovingfun

Social Media for Direct Selling Representatives *changed the way we look at social media and how we make it work for us. Direct Sales leaders wanted more and Karen answered. Her new book,* Social Media for Direct Selling Leaders *will be the #1 tool for leaders everywhere.*

Whether you are a new leader or an experienced leader, this book will transform how you lead your team and business.
Amy Riley, Norfolk VA
LuLaRoe Independent Fashion Retailer & Coach
facebook.com/lularoeamyriley

Contained within Social Media for Direct Selling Leaders *is a well laid out series of practical business-boosting social media tips. Covering all of the most-used platforms, this book contains a vast range of ideas with material suitable for all experience levels. I have saved multiple bookmarks of ideas I want to implement right away!*
Alison McLaughlin, Sarnia ON Canada
Keep Collective Founding Senior Designer
keepcollective.com/with/friday

Social Media for Direct Selling Leaders *is a great set of guidelines to help you navigate the social media world and use it to enhance your business. The advice Karen shares is invaluable and I would strongly recommend this book to anyone — from a brand-new consultant to an experienced director. I thought I was very social-media savvy, but even I learned quite a few new things from this book. This is an invaluable resource that every direct seller should have handy for reference. I can't wait to start implementing all the tips and tricks I've learned for my own team.*
Diana Duchscherer, Prince George BC Canada
Pampered Chef Team Leader
pamperedchef.biz/duchdi

Finally! A PLAYBOOK to propel my business. This is a must-have tool to grow an organization and to develop stronger connections through social media. As a leader with a global team, Karen has saved me hours of research by detailing step-by-step best practices to expand and connect with my team members, locally and worldwide. Simple and concise, this book teems with inspiration and new innovative ideas essential for our digital media age.

Maurita Tollestrup, Raymond AB Canada
Independent Scentsy Superstar Director
besmelly.com

My direct sales team is scattered across the whole country, which is a real challenge for me as a Manager. Karen's innovative and creative ideas for using social media have really changed how I support and build my team, especially with Live video. Best of all, I am using the social media platforms my team members already use in their own businesses and in their social lives. Just as Karen's first book harnessed the power of social media to connect consultants and customers, her new book now does the same for managers and their sales teams.

Andrew Humphrey, London England
Independent Tupperware Manager
facebook.com/thetupperwareman

This book will change the way I approach my business on social media. I thought I was fairly knowledgeable about the platforms I use, but I'm learning so many things from Karen Clark. The step-by-step approach that she clearly lays out for every platform and for each tool is simple to follow and makes me think, "Why didn't I do that before?!" Her approach makes the complex seem simple, and the easy-to-read format makes this book a must read for every direct sales consultant!

Boni Rish, Lloydminster AB Canada
Group Director, Steeped Tea
mysteepedtea.com/BoniRish

SOCIAL MEDIA
FOR DIRECT SELLING
Leaders

SOCIAL MEDIA
FOR DIRECT SELLING
Leaders

Growing and Supporting Your Team Online

KAREN CLARK

Connections Press
Rohnert Park, California

Connections Press
PO Box 1264
Rohnert Park, CA 94927

Publishing Website: connectionspress.com

Book Website: socialmediafordirectselling.com

General Website: mybusinesspresence.com
Email: karen@mybusinesspresence.com

Phone: 707-939-5709

Cover design by Angie Alaya, Pro eBook Covers
Cover illustration ©photoraidz/depositphotos.com
Author headshot by Blink, Inc. Corte Madera, CA

Book midwife, final edit, interior layout design:
Ruth Schwartz, mybookmidwife.com

Ordering Information:
Special discounts are available on quantity purchases by corporations, associations and others. For details, contact the "Special Sales Department" at the above address.

Social Media for Direct Selling Leaders / Karen Clark — 1st ed.
ISBN: 978-0-9971016-3-8 paperback
ISBN: 978-0-9971016-5-2 hardcover
ISBN: 978-0-9971016-4-5 ebook editions
Library of Congress Control Number: 2017905083

For my parents, George and Sandi,
whose unconditional support
enabled me to pursue my dreams!

Table of Contents

Introduction

I magine getting a phone call from somebody you had never met, telling you that they were in the area and would like to come and see you because your name kept showing up on their direct sales company's downline report.

I'll never forget the day that Lucy Brown called me. It was probably early 1999 and I was living in Washington State. I had joined my direct selling company back in September in Florida. Shortly thereafter my US Navy husband (at the time) got transferred up to Portland, Oregon. In between starting a new business, with two small children in tow, and moving clear across the country just about as far as you can get, I started building an organization of teams all across the United States due to some creative thinking and my consistent activity on the Internet.

By the time I got that call from Lucy, I was on a roll and on my way to being considered as a company pick for what we called the Inner Circle — a group of leaders who were invited to give the company input on new products and receive insider information. The funny thing is that within about a week of calling, Lucy, who had lived in Dana Point, California near San Diego at the time, actually drove up to Washington, knocked on my door and visited me. I did not really know her at that time — other than a few conversations on the phone — and she did not really know me or my history, but she certainly had noticed my swift and early success in the company.

I didn't know then, but Lucy was the number one director in the company and had a very large organization. When I joined I think she barely even noticed, and assumed that whoever sponsored me was supporting me, like we do when you have a large organization. Beyond a couple of generations down, you're assuming that downline leaders are taking care of their new people.

She did not know that was not true. Shortly after joining the company, the person who sponsored me jumped ship to another company. Since I did not even know how direct selling really worked, I did not seek out an upline leader for support. I just figured I was on my own. I started reading the manual, connecting with people for home parties in person and then began networking online once we found out we were being transferred. It all happened pretty quickly so I do not blame her for not reaching out earlier.

Once Lucy and I did connect, we became instant friends. Having been a military wife and living in Florida, far away from my family in Northern California, I missed being around family, and Lucy became somewhat of a surrogate mother to me who called me on a regular basis. I had been struggling in my marriage, overwhelmed with new motherhood, and eager to be the best consultant I could be so that I could continue to stay home with my two girls without needing to return to teaching school.

Lucy saw something in me I did not even see. She saw someone creative, innovative and determined. I was the type of team member that every direct selling leader craves. I was coachable, a self-starter, and passionate about the products. Lucy immediately looped me into her team newsletter, which was still on paper at that time, and called me to coach me on a regular basis. She made sure I was involved in company training calls and events and that I got along and was accepted by the other leaders.

I rose so quickly in my company that the veterans of this over 30-year-old business did not know what hit them! In fact when I did go to that inner circle retreat, I was met with skepticism — rightfully so — from those who had spent years and years building their businesses. They wondered what my secret was, and were a little anxious that someone so new could achieve levels that they had earned through blood, sweat and tears! They thought that I was too good to be true, or that I was somehow cheating, or taking shortcuts.

Nothing could be further from the truth! I was what you might call an accidental leader. I fell in love with the products, told everyone I knew about them, and booked home parties right and left. The next thing I knew, I was taking it to the Internet and sponsoring people all over the United States based on the relationships I was building as I connected with them through the early days of social media.

Although I had little understanding of the direct selling business model when I started, I had always been one to give 110 percent to all that I do. In my early months in the business I did not have the support of a leader, and I was determined to offer that to people that I brought in — starting with the very first one. I knew what it was like to do things on my own and although it did not deter me, I knew that once I did connect with Lucy, my business expanded and I was ultimately tapped to take on the corporate position of Director of Consultant Development, providing support and training to the entire company.

Very early in my career—and out of necessity—I started implementing ways to connect with my team across the United States. First there were weekly phone calls and then monthly paper newsletters, and later there were e-groups, forums and chat rooms. Later still there were weekly meetings via chats, webinars, training and support via YouTube videos, virtual accountability partners, and all day online rallies complete with guest trainers. Others in the industry started calling me a pioneer. No one had really done this online at this scale before, but due to my comfort level with technology, it just seemed natural to me!

I can honestly say that growing and supporting a direct selling team has been one of the most fulfilling careers of my life. Not because of the money that I made or even the friendships that I was able to develop, but because of the difference I was able to make in peoples lives the way Lucy did for me. Let me explain.

As you read in my first book, when I took my business to the Internet I was able to connect with people around the country and find support for what was then a troubled marriage. I felt alone and struggled with the lack of connection when I did not even have that from my own husband at home. Developing as a leader in direct sales was so empowering for me as an individual that it enabled me to not only stay home with my kids, which was my first priority, but also to give me a voice to express myself, which led to the confidence to ask for what I want in life and actually dream and achieve.

Before becoming a leader, I married young and my identity was so tied up in my children and my marriage that there really was no Karen anymore. Finding success in direct sales gave me a way to find myself again and to realize that I am important to people, that I am smart, that I am worthy of success — and deserve to be treated well. Having a steady income that I earned on my own gave me the financial freedom to be able to say, "I'm done." After living with an alcoholic for most of my marriage, and then discovering that he was having affairs, I had had enough.

The day I attended my grandmother's funeral and realized that I would probably live to be about her age (she lived to her mid-eighties), I came to the conclusion that the life I had been living with my husband, with the lack of trust and the disrespect, would more than likely continue until the day I died, fifty years forward. I returned from her funeral determined to start a new chapter in my life. Without my direct selling business, and the organization that I had grown, there would have been no way out of the situation I was in.

Being a direct selling leader gave me freedom: freedom to create a better life for my daughters; freedom to begin earning back my own self-respect that had been eroded over the 15 years of marriage; freedom to move back to California and surround myself with family; freedom to ultimately meet my new forever-husband and provide for my girls and our new son together.

Leaders, when you hear people say that direct selling changes people's lives, it is not just lip service. When you grow and support your own team, you empower others who may need to get out of a bad situation as well. Technology enables leaders to reach people all across the country and to provide support that strengthens resolve, empowers dreams and provides an income for them to get what they are really needing in life. Not everybody has a sad story or an overwhelming challenge to overcome, but everyone has goals and dreams to create a better life for themselves in the world.

My hope is that the tips and techniques I discuss in this book, which by and large are based on my actual experience both as a top direct selling leader and as an industry expert in technology, will empower you to empower others. My journey as a leader was incredible, based in large part on the tactics I employed that connected my team to each other and to me on a regular basis, helped them feel supported, and provided the training they needed so that they could make changes in their lives.

In recent years I have been working with companies and top leaders to fine-tune my tactics and update them based on current social media platforms and best practices. It is my pleasure to provide this information to you in hopes that you too can truly change people's lives with your support. Lucy has since retired from direct sales, but she has never stopped inspiring me to support, encourage and empower others. When your heart is deeply invested in this business and you truly care for the success of others, it's contagious!

How to Use This Book

Before you dive into the following chapters, I wanted to be sure we are all on the same page, so to speak, about a few things. This book is designed to be a supplement to my first book in the series, *Social Media for Direct Selling Representatives* — not to be used independently. The reason for this is that, in order to most effectively carry out the strategies within, it is important that you have a good understanding of my underlying principles. Throughout this edition you will find I reference **the first book in the series, which I assume you already have read.** If you happen to have come across this edition without having already read the first book, I suggest you do that now.

This book was written with the independent direct selling leader in mind. Whether you are a leader of one or a leader of many, an industry veteran, an "accidental leader" or a future leader, you will find value in this book. I am covering some basics as well as content that even the most experienced leader can use.

Although some of the principles apply to general business entrepreneurs, the intended audience is made up of the individual business owners in leadership positions in the direct selling industry. As such, there are a few distinctions you might notice.

About Direct Selling

Direct selling representatives are independent consultants, distributors or business owners who represent a direct selling company. There is some confusion about what constitutes direct selling, but for the purpose of this book and my readers, direct selling is the business model where a company allows independent contractors to sign an agreement to sell the company's products for a commission, working as an independent representative, sometimes directly with customers (one on one) and sometimes in a group demonstration or party environment. There is a multi-tiered pay plan that allows the representative to also get a percentage of the sales garnered by someone that they introduce the business to who also signs up, and any additional people who are enrolled by that person. At the time the representative enrolls a person in the business, they could be considered a direct selling leader, though most companies have specific requirements to officially achieve various leadership levels and titles.

Within the business designation of "direct sales" there are two basic models: Party Plan and Network Marketing/MLM. Technically person-to-person sales, such as door-to-door selling, is also a direct selling or direct sales option, but is far less typical and operates very differently than what we are discussing in this book.

Party Plan representatives typically conduct the vast majority of their business by selling products through group gatherings known as home parties, shows or gatherings, and by bringing others into the business. They may also choose to sell through online parties or virtual shows, which are also group situations. In these gatherings, there is often a separate person who acts as the host and invites his or her friends to attend the demonstration or sales talk. The host is then rewarded with free or discounted product in exchange for introducing the product to people she knows. Although Party Plan representatives also sell product in other settings — such as vendor fairs, craft shows, fundraisers, one-on-one appointments and more — the primary business model is selling to a group of individuals at one time, either in person or online. The emphasis with Party Plan companies is on product sales as well as introducing interested customers and hosts to the income opportunity. Therefore, there are often seasonal, annual or bi-annual new product introductions, monthly product specials and monthly exclusive product for hosts.

Network Marketing/MLM representatives generally conduct most of their business through networking one-on-one, through word of mouth and through referrals from the people they meet. Networking with other individuals is key, and doing so in person or by phone, online or through other communication methods is most common, although some Network Marketing representatives also like to set up group demonstrations, tastings and informational events. Network Marketing representatives are paid commission on the sale of their products as well as for enrolling both customers and business builders in the business. In recently years, however, there has been a shift toward rewarding product sales to outside customers. In the most common pay plans, there are typically a variety of incentives to bring on additional representatives, building a large team of people that will also begin enrolling others.

Who Was this Book Written For?

Much of this book is directed to both Party Plan and Network Marketing/MLM representatives and I welcome people from both business models to take the advice that appeals to them the most.

Since the majority of direct selling representatives—and therefore leaders—are female, I have decided to use the pronouns "she" and "her" throughout the book, even though I recognize that there are many male representatives and leaders as well. Rather than alternate between male and female, I made the call to go with female for the purposes of my books.

Other labels you may see in this book would be the terms used for representatives and leaders. Companies vary in their titles and you may find I varied my terminology as well. Consultants or distributors are labels I typically use for representatives. Leader or Director are typical labels for leaders who are building and supporting a team.

Stay in Compliance

Since you are more than likely a direct selling leader (or aspiring leader) reading this book, I'd like to mention that the chapters were written in a general way to apply to anyone in direct sales. The advice is not company-specific and your own company may have guidelines that differ from mine. Staying in compliance with your company's policy is vital, so please keep that in mind. I work with many companies and have attempted to accommodate most, but there are some I'm unfamiliar with. I cannot take responsibility for you taking actions that may not be in alignment with your company. Always check with your Policies & Procedures or with the home office directly if you aren't sure whether something is allowed. It is up to you to cross check with your company, or even suggest policy changes if you find they could use some updating. This is not unheard of.

Mobile vs. Desktop

Mobile marketing is the wave of the future and most people now are connected to their mobile device during every waking hour. It is as if you have a computer in your pocket and we seem to have a hard time living without them! That said, as a direct selling leader who plans to put some intentional time into marketing your business through social media, you will probably do much of it from your home office. Although you will, of course, be ready to respond and possibly post from your smart phone as needed, I imagine you are like me and have set times to work on your marketing in a stationary spot. For this reason, most of the instructions included in this book assume you are using the desktop version of the applications we are discussing. If I were to include both desktop and mobile instructions I would need to make this a much longer book, so I decided to go with the desktop version for most platforms, except for Instagram and Facebook Live, which are at this time primarily mobile applications.

Bonus Resources

Social media platforms, best practices, and technology shift very rapidly, and sometimes without warning. If you've ever opened your Facebook to see things completely rearranged, you know what I am talking about! As you can imagine, writing a book about social media and Internet marketing is challenging for this reason. There is always a risk that by the time my readers receive their books, something will be out-of-date.

Social media is always evolving. To help keep up with changes that may occur, I've created a special Resource Page for anyone who has purchased this book in the same way that I did for the first book, *Social Media for Direct Selling Representatives*. By first registering for our private resource page using the link below, you will have the opportunity to receive updates to any of these chapters as well as bonus material that will help you further implement what you learn in this book.

Register here with your contact information to receive the link and password to our resource page for this book and then check your email:
smdsbook.com/resources2

Modeling for Your Team

Know Your Starting Point

Do you know where you stand when it comes to using social media as a direct seller or leader? Many entrepreneurs feel that they are sort of wandering aimlessly out there, hoping something works, especially direct sales representatives using social media. You feel like you "should," so you do, but you aren't really sure you are doing it "right" or even sure you are getting results. This can be even more pronounced if you are a leader with many other obligations in your business besides the day to day connecting, selling, scheduling sales events or sponsoring.

Knowing where you are now can help you determine what to do next, or where you can improve. In the assessment below, put a checkmark in the boxes that describe areas where you already feel like you are "nailing it" in social media, and then put an asterisk where you might need some help or just aren't sure. If you are somewhat new to social media, you will get an idea of what you may want to put in place as you move forward. If you are a social media pro, you may see areas for improvement.

My Social Media Platforms

☐ I have a strong customer-facing presence on Facebook via a Business Page.

☐ I have a complete LinkedIn profile with my business information added, using keywords that will attract my prospects.

☐ I automate when necessary or when it makes sense to further engagement, such as I may have my Facebook set to post to Twitter, occasionally cross-post from other platforms, or schedule posts when I am away.

☐ On Pinterest, I have an appropriate mix of business and personal boards and pins.

☐ I use Instagram to post photographs "in the moment" throughout my week.

☐ I understand and adhere to the rules and regulations the platforms have set regarding utilizing social media for business vs. personal use.

☐ I regularly receive likes, replies and shares of my social media posts.

☐ My verbiage and visual branding are in alignment with my personal and business values.

☐ I feel I am well-trained and confident in professionally using social media.

☐ I attend social media training at our company live events whenever possible.

☐ I have read and understand our company's social media policies and always comply, regardless of what I see others doing.

☐ I am aware of appropriate resources and tools I can turn to for additional help with social media.

☐ I regularly receive leads that convert to sales and sponsoring due to my social media efforts.

☐ My customers regularly reach out to me via social media with questions or to re-order.

☐ I participate in social media on a daily basis while not neglecting other business-building activities.

Social Media as a Leader

☐ I have a semi-private social media site, group or blog for team support and community building.

☐ I enjoy creating pre-recorded and live video to personally connect with my team or prospects, creating closer connections to them.

☐ I know how to conduct effective public opportunity events online in a way that gets results.

☐ As a leader, I include social media topics in the regular support/training I provide.

☐ I feel confident in passing along social media best practices to my new team members.

☐ I have sponsored in new geographical locations due to a prospect discovering me through social media.

☐ I model for my team positive and professional online behavior both in public forums and in internal or company groups.

☐ I provide ongoing training and support for my team in the area of technology or social media.

How did you do? Do you see what you might want to learn next? For the foundational education on your own social media platform use, I recommend checking out my first book, *Social Media for Direct Selling Representatives,* and its bonus resources, or perhaps my private support group, Karen on Call.

For information on using social media as a direct selling leader, continue to read the next chapters in this book and you will learn how to expand your personal expertise in using the platforms to build your business and in supporting your team.

Polishing Your Platforms

If you have read my first book, *Social Media for Direct Selling Representatives*, you learned some general best practices for each of the most popular social media sites, and if you accessed the Resources Page, you also were able to follow step-by-step instructions for setting up each platform. As a leader, it is time to step things up a bit and set yourself up not only to attract and support new team members, but also to set an example of professionalism for everyone in your organization, your company and the direct selling profession at large.

In this chapter I will share some tips for increasing the effectiveness of your social media platforms as a leader, focusing not only on modeling for your team, but on building your organization.

If you recall in the first book, I do not recommend that everyone use every social media site out there, but that you instead focus on one platform, do it well, and perhaps then move on to another. The idea is to do one thing skillfully and not spread yourself too thin. As a leader this approach is one of the best things you can model for your team since social media is very alluring. It is tempting for you and your team members to create a presence everywhere! More is better, right? Not really. Managing your time is an important skill, too, in order to achieve lasting success and longevity in your business. See my chapter on <u>Social Media Time Savers</u> for more information. Meanwhile, here are some

Tips for Polishing Each Platform

Whichever site you use, try these strategies and tactics for increasing its effectiveness for you as a leader, making more of an impact and getting quality results.

Facebook

If you have created a Facebook Business Page (which you should have!) edit your About section on your Personal Profile so that in the Work and Education section it lists your business page as your current "workplace." This makes it easy for people to find out what you do and click directly over to your Business Page if they are your friends, or someone who simply comes across your profile in other ways such as in Facebook Groups or by reading comments you may have made on other profiles or pages.

Likewise, check to make sure you have made your business information and website link "public" and not set to "friends only" within your Basic Information. By default, these things are visible only to your Facebook friends, but when it comes to networking for business, it is important to make it easy for others to contact you. To change the privacy of your work information and website, visit your profile's About tab and then click Contact and Basic Info on the left. As you hover your mouse over the right side you will be able to click on the pencil icon to edit. Then find the privacy icon, which might look like a lock, a silhouette or a globe. For any item you would like to be visible to the public, click to drop down on the icon to change it to the globe/public.

I recommend doing this on your phone number and email address as well, since having that information available adds a level of credibility. If you are nervous about having your personal email address and phone number on social media, try creating new ones just for use on your online platforms. I like to use a free Google Voice number that I can then set to forward to another personal number or have incoming calls go to voicemail. Go to google.com/voice to get a free phone number. The same is true for your email address. Create a separate email address just for social media use, such as karenclark-social@gmail.com. If you are using Gmail, it is easy to go into the settings and have that email address forward to another one without revealing your primary email address to your contacts.

Be sure to include your face in your profile image — people respond and feel more connected to a headshot vs. product images or the cover of your catalog! In your Business Page's cover image or banner, try using an image that reflects either the business opportunity or a feeling of business success or working from home, or something that gives the viewer a sense of what it would be like to be on your team. I heard someone once say that your income opportunity is your best product! Don't be shy about sharing it visually in some way. Just make sure you are in compliance with your company's P&P regarding branding and images.

Be sure you have turned on the Call to Action button on your business page. This will create a Shop Now, or Sign Up, or Learn More button that you can redirect to your personal website when someone clicks on it.

Set up or adjust your Username to reflect your name and/or product. By default, Facebook includes your full page name and a Page ID (numbers) in the URL of your page. This is quite cumbersome. By setting a Username you can choose which keywords you would like in your URL, which makes your Facebook link easier to share. If you have a personal brand or team name, you can use that. Using a combination of your real name and the type of product you offer works well also. For example mine might be @karensprettypurses, which then creates the Page URL facebook.com/karensprettypurses. Check your company policy for rules about your Username or Facebook URL. Most companies do not allow you to use the company branded names in your URL.

Create a contact form tab on your Business Page using something like JotForm.com. You can insert checkboxes so that people can request business information. This will show up as a navigation link on the left side of your page. When someone fills out your form, you have permission to contact them individually or to add them to your newsletter or other emails.

Join Facebook Groups where your prospects might be hanging out. Be of service. Comment on posts without promoting your business—unless asked. Post your own discussion questions. Let people get to know you.

If you have a large customer or party host base, consider starting your own VIP group for customers—your best customers and hosts are your hottest prospects. Within the group you can get to know each other, share ideas, discuss related topics and share exclusive or new information or product releases. Note that Facebook Groups are not a place to sell product; they are intended for discussion only, since they can only be administered by personal profiles. When you have something "salesy" you would like to share with your VIP group, first post it to your Business Page and then share that post to your group to avoid the possibility of landing in "Facebook Jail" for using a profile for business.

If you do in-home parties, after each party invite the host and guests to "like" your Business Page. You can do this via email, texting or through a private Facebook message, though they may not receive it if you are not Facebook friends. Be sure to customize each message so Facebook does not perceive it as spam. Copying and pasting is really not a good idea anyway, so personalize each message. Invite them to your Business Page by including the link to it in your private message and let them know you'd love to stay connected to them on Facebook! If you are with them in person, it is also fun to simply ask them to like your page, show you that they have done so on their phones, and thank them in some way, such as with a small discount on their order or entries into a drawing.

On Facebook, when you have a Business Page, you can interact with other business pages as your own business page (instead of from your Personal Profile). Search for other pages that cater to working from home, stay-at-home moms, entrepreneurial women and so on. Interact on those pages (in a non-promotional way) as your page by clicking your small profile icon just under the post, on the right. Change that profile picture in the drop-down menu to the one from your Business Page. From there, you can like and comment on the post and your business name will show up, exposing your page to the people who liked the page of the original poster. Note that this only works on other businesses, not personal profiles or groups.

Consider placing a paid ad customized to your ideal demographic if your company allows paid advertising on Facebook. Or try a paid "Boosted" post where you pay a small amount (as low as $1 if you click "Choose your own amount") to make sure a specific post on your Business Page is seen by more people.

LinkedIn

LinkedIn is where people go to find jobs, gain referrals for jobs, or find ways to augment their income. It is a perfect place to grow your team, yet it is an often under-utilized platform. Most people today have a LinkedIn profile, but do not use it unless they are actively seeking work. Those who are actively seeking work are prospects for you. Out of all the social platforms out there, it makes the most sense to use LinkedIn to attract new team members, rather than customers. People do not use LinkedIn to shop for products.

It is important that you use a clear and professional head-shot photo on LinkedIn for your profile image. In addition, you also have an opportunity to share a banner image that stretches across the back of your profile. This is a very large image, which displays differently on mobile vs. desktop, so keeping it as simple as possible works well so that it looks great on all de-vices. I've seen people use company-provided images but I've also seen people use scenery from the area in which they live and that is a nice option too. It does not have to be about your specific business either. There are simple graphic background images you can get on the Internet from royalty-free image sources that work as well.

Make sure your LinkedIn profile reflects that you are look-ing for business partners, or that you are offering an income opportunity. Include good keywords in your summary and other descriptions that make it clear to readers that you are a leader in the position of offering them an opportunity to earn an income in the company you are in. One of the biggest mis-takes I see on LinkedIn are profiles that are not leveraging the use of the word count you are allowed to include. Not only does using good keywords in your profile and summaries help you get found in the search engines if your privacy settings allow your profile to be visible (which it should!) but within LinkedIn itself, people often search for certain topics, people, locations or positions. The only way LinkedIn knows whose profile to suggest in the search results are the words you include.

As an experiment, choose a topic you would like to be known for and that people might search for. For me, it might be "direct selling speaker" or "social media trainer." So I would type those into the search box at the top of the LinkedIn home page. For you it might be "home-based business opportunity" or "makeup business" or jewelry business" or "work at home." The simpler the better, as the goal is to use words people who are not already associated with your business might use in their search. Try searching on a phrase like that and see who comes up in the search results within the top five. Look at their LinkedIn profiles and read through to see where those words appear. Often you will see they have naturally included that phrase multiple times in their summary and work experience descriptions. You can do the same. Making sure your topic words are included in several places makes a difference in how you can be found on LinkedIn.

Consider adding a Media section and possibly a Project section to your profile. You do this by clicking on the small square with a + symbol when you are in Edit Profile mode. In the media area you can add images, PDFs or videos about anything you would like to highlight, but as a leader it would make sense to add information about your income opportunity. For projects, LinkedIn will prompt you to add a project and within that area you can indicate you are seeking business partners.

Then link the project to the appropriate page on your website. The project section is great because it links directly from the title of the project that you create to any page on your website that you choose. See my chapter, LinkedIn for Leaders, for more specific ideas for how to use LinkedIn's features.

Twitter

Twitter is known for sharing information in short spurts. Your tweets can only consist of up to 140 characters including any links, and the bio in your profile can only include up to 160 characters. Find a way to succinctly let people know what you do and that you are looking for new team members. Simple phrases like "Help Wanted" or "Ground Floor Opportunity" work well, in addition to a general bio about you or your business.

Again, you will want to use a headshot image and a larger banner. In the settings on Twitter you are also able to adjust the "design" of your Twitter page to have your fonts and background colors more closely resemble your company's or your own branded colors if you wish.

Twitter's search is powerful. Try searching on "I want to work from home" or "How can I make money at home" and see what comes up. Do the same by typing in a hashtag such as #bizopp (business opportunity) or #wahm (work at home Mom) into the search bar. Using Twitter's built-in search can be a great way to connect with people looking for something you provide, including your business opportunity.

Consider conducting a business opportunity event using Twitter and a hashtag you create. Invite your contacts, and perhaps your team and their contacts, to join you at a certain time on Twitter following that hashtag. You can then carry out an opportunity event similar to the one I mention in the chapter,

<u>Online Opportunity Events</u>. You would simply be "tweeting" the questions and comments, adding pictures, videos or links where appropriate, and following along either in the search for your hashtag, or using a tool such as <u>TweetChat.com</u> or <u>Twubs.com</u> to keep things organized. Since Twitter is public, your posts will go to the feed of your followers, but this isn't usually a problem on Twitter, which can tolerate more frequent posts. In fact you may generate some interest among those you did not know might be interested!

Pinterest

As with the other social media platforms, on Pinterest you will want to make sure you are mostly posting non-promotional items, so be sure to "pin" lots of different things in addition to business information. Let people get to know you as a person by sharing things you are interested in. Once in a while pin something about your business or an article from your blog, if you have one.

As you review your Pinterest account, boards and pins, make sure each has its own description set up with good key-words that others may be searching for. Pinterest is a powerful discovery site and many people find new things to try through the search within Pinterest, but this is only possible if the words they are looking for appear on each item.

Consider starting a Pinterest board about working from home in general, or direct selling tips in general. View this as a library of bookmarks people will want to access regularly. You will quickly be seen as an authority.

To support your team, start a "secret" Pinterest board and invite your team members to contribute to it. From there you can all post items your team can either use and learn from themselves, or items everyone can share to their own networks. This can act as a nice resource library of post ideas to share.

I am frequently asked whether to create a business account on Pinterest and I do believe this would be beneficial to anyone in direct sales. That said, having your account designated as a business account does not mean it is best to only post about your business. I recommend still having many other boards on a variety of topics, and a few that are specific to your business. The advantage of using a business account is that Pinterest provides very thorough Insights — or analytics — only to business accounts. I recommend keeping your account in your own name, with a link to your website. Readers are more likely to trust your recommendations and share your posts if there is a personal connection.

Instagram

Instagram is quickly rising as a popular platform for the general population. Therefore, it is a great place to meet new people and build up a following of folks who will interact with you. No longer only a photo-sharing app among friends, there's power in hashtags on Instagram. I like to add three to five to every post. See the chapter on Hashtags for Direct Selling for some suggestions. If you search or tap on any of the hashtags you chose, you will find even more hashtags attached to posts within each category.

Remember that Instagram is a photo-sharing site, so do not go overboard with detailed graphics and posts with lots of words on them. Whenever possible, focus on compliant lifestyle pictures on Instagram and not marketing graphics.

If your team is using Instagram, consider setting up a separate account for yourself as a leader that they can subscribe to, where you send inspirational images or quick videos that would show up in their feed. Instagram allows you to switch between multiple accounts (up to four) on the mobile app, which makes it easy to create additional business accounts and keep your personal Instagram account separate.

Instagram contests can be very effective in drawing new people to your account and generating interest. See the chapter on <u>Instagram Contests</u> in the section on <u>Growing Your Team</u>.

Direct selling is a relationship business and relationships take time. Do you want a long-lasting relationship or a one-night stand? Be the kind of person that people want to do business with and you will draw the right people to you like a magnet. If you push and pull at them to do what you want, you will be pushing and pulling them (or worse, dragging them) throughout their whole careers! The keys are to draw people in, take action consistently and keep your pipeline full of prospects.

Focus on Facebook Best Practices

As you learned in my first book, Social Media CPR is a social media activity formula I recommend that allows you to be more effective online in less time. I thought it would be a good idea to refresh your memory, since saving time is so important for leaders who want to have a successful business—and a life! Social Media CPR stands for Comment, Post, Reply. This is a system I devised because I needed a way to save time and get off the computer and back to work. Here are some general tips for using it, along with other smart tasks on Facebook:

Personal Facebook Account

1. **Comment** on three to five posts (other people's—not yours) as your Personal Profile or your Business Page. Just scroll through the news feed and find some posts that resonate with you; either put in your own two cents or just add a quick comment on the post, photo, video or link that others have shared. When appropriate @tag in the comment if replying to a specific person within the comment thread.

2. If you know you are using your personal Facebook for networking and relationship building, **post** something new to your personal timeline profile (as yourself), but no more than two or three times a day. Many people, like myself, do use a Personal Profile for connections but prefer to post only occasionally, two or three times per week or whenever we are inspired to, and that is okay too. Posts on your Personal Profile should provide a window for your connections to see who you are, what you do (without a sales pitch), activities you're involved in, things that inspire you and so on. Vary your posts between plain text status updates, photos, links to things you find interesting, and videos whenever possible. The more variety of post types that you use, the better for Facebook's algorithm, which is constantly changing.

3. **Reply** during or at the end of the day to any comments left on your Facebook wall or posts so that others who have commented earlier see that you are hands-on, present and reading the comments. Your goal is to be the last person to comment. Check your notifications or simply scroll down the last couple day's worth of wall posts to check who has the last comment.

   - Check for any private messages that may need to be responded to on your personal account and handle them.

   - Accept any appropriate friend requests, and consider using the Add to List feature according to whatever industry, region or other group that would be meaningful to sort people into to help you stay organized. To decide, think of any demographic you may want a specific post or event or message to go to—such as *direct sellers, vendors, media,* etc. This will enable you to customize who sees what when you click the little button on posts or in privacy settings. It is important to note that you do not need to feel obligated to "friend" everyone on your team or within your company. In fact, as your business grows you may regret this! If you are truly friends, it's nice to keep in touch but it's also okay to simply leave them as a Follower or to add them to the Restricted or Acquaintance list. Note that, if you are friends with someone and unfriend them, they stay on as a Follower of your public posts, as long as you have that feature turned on in your privacy settings.

- Reply or remove any event invitations. This will reduce unwanted emails and notifications. If you reply "Can't go" or click the X next to the event, it will remove you and the event admin won't contact you with reminders any more.

- Check into any outside Groups you may have joined (find the Groups tab on the left side of your Home page) and scan or reply to anything where you might want to add your two cents or ask a question, such as in your company's consultant or leaders group. I strongly recommend you consider limiting your activity in other Facebook Groups as they tend to be very time consuming—almost addicting! Many of them are filled with drama and do not help you build your business. If you are using them to network or promote your business, it's a good idea to check once in a while, but this does not need to be a daily task.

Facebook Business Page

1. **Comment** on three to five posts on other Business Pages as your own Business Page. Do this by finding the small profile image of yourself on the business page's posts and click to switch it to commenting as your Business Page. Scroll through the news feed and find some posts that resonate with you and add a meaningful comment. If you aren't already connected to other business pages you can use the search bar to find some to comment on. You do not need to have "liked" the page to comment on it as your Business Page.

2. **Post** something new to your own Business Page at least once but no more than three or four times a day. Twice is ideal—early in the day and a bit later. Posts on your Business Page should be educational, helpful, useful or inspirational items that your target market would appreciate learning, reflecting on or discovering. Limit direct marketing items to about 10 percent of all posts as outlined in my 9-1-1 Code from *Social Media for Direct Selling Representatives* (less is more.) Focus on sharing ideas, asking questions, sharing quotes, events, articles, how-tos, news and so on that is relevant. Vary your posts between text status updates, photos, links to relevant articles elsewhere on the Internet and videos—including Facebook Live whenever possible. The more variety the better!

3. **Reply** during or at the end of the day to any comments left on the Business Page wall, status updates/links/photos/videos so that others who have commented before see that you are hands-on and present, and reading the comments. Your goal is for you, as your Business Page, to be the last person to comment in a thread of conversation. Check your page notifications

36

or simply scroll down the last couple day's worth of wall posts to see who has the last comment.

4. After you have earned some "likes" on your posts, click the list of people who liked the post and you will see a panel of people's names next to a button that says either Invite, Liked or Invited. If they liked your individual post but have not liked the page itself, the Invite button will be active and you can easily invite them to like your page from there. I recommend doing this a couple times a week and it will increase your overall page likes significantly.

5. Check your Business Page's Inbox at least daily, or as messages come in. This is very important for customer service!

6. Check your Insights tab. Take mental note of positive or negative activity in general, then click on any section to see details. Under Posts see which ones have the highest percentage of engagement. This can inform you as to which types of posts are successful. Therefore you might want to do more of some and less of others.

7. Invite people to your Business Page by individual email addresses or a CSV spreadsheet. Go to your page and under the 3 dots near your cover image click on Suggest Page to access the features of inviting by email. You will be able to upload a CSV or other contact file through here, and invites will be sent out to everyone on that list.

8. Invite new Facebook friends to like your page by opening up your Friends tab on your Personal Profile in one window, clicking on the Recently Added section, and then opening the Invite Friends tab from your Business Page in another. On your Invite Friends tab from your page, type in the names of your new Facebook friends to invite them to

your page, if appropriate. I do this about once a week, since many people will friend me but are really interested in my business information. The same will probably be true for you, except in the case of your own team or company representatives. See *Social Media for Direct Selling Representatives* to see why I do not recommend direct sellers like each others' business pages if in the same company. It can actually hurt your business!

Your Facebook Groups

As with your Personal Profile and Business Pages on Facebook, if you choose to use a Facebook Group either for VIP customers or hosts, or for your team, it is important to regularly engage with the group members. I recommend posting once per day, but not too much more than that. Since notifications are automatic in groups, frequent posting can be overwhelming to your members. Of course, it is also important to respond and interact within others' posts and comments within each group.

Social Media CPR and the 9-1-1 Code apply to your team Facebook Groups as well. Comment on three to five posts within the group, post something new, and reply to anything directed to you. This process should take about a half hour a day. Comment, Post, Reply.

If you find that you are spending much more time than that on a daily basis, take a look at how you are "training" your team to treat the group. Remember that your goal as a leader is to teach your team to be resourceful and empowered to run their own business, not to rely on you for answers that they could find on their own.

If you find you are answering the same questions over and over again, be sure to start referring them to past posts or trainings, or where they can find that answer in your company's guidebook or back office. This isn't so they don't feel support-ed—it *is* supporting them by teaching them to find their own answers.

The types of questions they can ask you in your group should be ones that can't be answered by the company manual or trainings. Rather, they should be looking for your opinion or advice based on your personal experience. See more about managing a team group in the chapter about Facebook Groups for Your Team.

Social Media Time Savers

I know what it is like to be a busy direct selling leader who is responsible for keeping your personal business going while also sponsoring new people into your team, onboarding them with new start training and support, and at the same time, coaching and training your existing team members and mentoring your future leaders. Some of you may also be a support person for directors within your own organization, or be juggling other responsibilities with the company such as being a member of the corporate advisory team. Add family life, your personal social circle and possibly a job outside the home and it's no wonder keeping up with social media feels overwhelming to some. It can be time consuming if you let it. In this chapter I will share some tips that help you streamline your social media use, which, in conjunction with remembering how to use Social Media CPR, will help you get online, get noticed, do your job as a leader, and get back offline!

Use Facebook Friend Lists
Organizing your Facebook friends into Friend Lists can help you manage your time and ensure your message gets delivered

to a targeted group of people when posting from your Personal Profile, when sharing from other pages to your personal friends, or when inviting people to events.

Facebook has done a great job explaining how to set up Friend Lists within their Help Center. I recommend you follow the instructions here: facebook.com/help/204604196335128.

I love how using Friend Lists allows me to ensure the messages I want to send publicly on my timeline go only to the people I know will be interested. With Facebook cracking down on spam, it is so important to customize any business-related messages to go only to lists of people who would be interested. Otherwise, some folks might inadvertently hurt your Facebook presence by hiding your posts or marking them as spam.

Create a Facebook Library of Training Ideas

If you are like most leaders using Facebook, you will often add an image to your posts in your team group to make it more visually appealing. By default, your image posts do not go into an Album but can be found simply in your group's Photos area, unsorted. However, you can choose to create albums as you upload, or you can visit the Photos and then Albums tab to add pictures to Albums. This is how to make your group's Photos tab a library of resources for your team based on topic! For example, on your Photos/Albums tab, you can have an Album called "Booking Parties" and another one called "Sponsoring" or even "Networking" or any other topic you train on. Then when you create a post about those topics they are easy to find later because you've placed it in the right album. Any time someone would like to refer to a past training, or when you have someone new come on board, it is easy to find the trainings and either share the link to the full album, or "tag" the person in the comments.

To do this, simply visit your Photos tab. If you do not have one yet, it will be created when you first upload a picture to your group. Sometimes you have to click More or Info at the end of your white tabs under your group's cover image. Create group albums before you even need them by first creating an image that has the title or topic of the group. Try using something like the image editing program Canva to create these images for each category such as "Vendor Events," "Party Games," "Seasonal Themes" or any training topic you know will come up several times. Upload your title picture that you created by clicking on the photo post and choosing Create an Album and then give your album a name and description. This will make it easier for you to be able to choose the right album any time you add new pictures. You can edit the album and its description any time. You can also go into any of the images you have posted in the past and edit their captions.

Now when you upload new images or trainings, you can stay organized by choosing to add them to the album you created (or create a new one when you upload). When someone visits your Photos tab and clicks on Albums, they will see a variety of topics organized into a nice Resource Library.

Schedule Your Posts

In my first book, *Social Media for Direct Selling Representatives,* one of the chapters outlines my thoughts and suggestions about automating social media (or not). I have to say, if ever there was an appropriate reason to schedule social media posts it is when you are a busy leader with lots of obligations to fulfill! Using time-saving tools is the only way I was able to juggle having a quickly expanding team across the USA, along with a busy personal business, being a mom to two young children and basically a single mother since my military husband was gone a lot! Later, after we separated, I was a single mother at the time when my business was booming the most so I know what it is like to juggle it all and need help any way you can get it. Luckily there are tools that enable you to be in two places at once.

On Facebook Business Pages, I always recommend using the native schedule button within the post publisher. Any time you can use Facebook's built-in tools you will find you get further reach and more consistent likes and comments on your posts. But for your team group or even your Personal Profile or events as needed, there are no built-in tools, so you need to look elsewhere. I personally use CinchShare for groups, my Personal Profile and Events within Facebook Groups or Business Pages, and it works great. I have also heard good things about other applications, such as Post My Party, that would work well for both parties and training. Not only are these tools easy to use, they were started by direct sellers who understand our business model and keep up with what we need. For other social media sites, such as LinkedIn, look into schedulers such as Buffer or Hootsuite.

Online Appointment Schedulers

Sometimes you may have an occasion to schedule a meeting, one on one coaching appointment, sponsoring interview or a group gathering with someone else. Rather than trying to catch all participants on the phone, or dealing with lots of emails back and forth, I've found it really helpful to use some online scheduling tools.

Some are free, some are paid, some include database storage, some include reminders, and some even include buttons for your website or Facebook page. Some are designed for booking one-on-one appointments, and others are ideal for scheduling groups. Some even allow you to take payments from your clients if that is appropriate for your business. Using these tools has allowed me to control my calendar more efficiently and book solid dates more quickly. I like the ones that allow you to embed them on your website or create a tab on your Facebook Page. Right now I am using Setmore for that reason. Every business is different and what appeals to one person may not appeal to another, so check these out and decide for yourself:

- Setmore

- Doodle

- Acuity Scheduling

- Time Trade

- Calendly

- Meet-o-Matic

- Google Calendar

- YouCanBook.Me

Email Time Savers

Technically this is not related to social media, but I think any time you can use technology to save time you should! With the popularity of using Google for email many extensions have come about that you can use with Google's Chrome browser. When I first learned of these I was hesitant—I had been a die-hard Firefox browser user for years and then later went back to Safari with my latest MacBook and really didn't want to have to start using Chrome just so I could access these tools. However, I can tell you today I am glad I finally did, and I think you will be too. It is worth switching browsers to be able to use these time-savers!

The first one that I love is called Boomerang. Boomerang allows you to do several things but the features I use most are the ability to write an email at any time day or night and schedule it to go out at a set time. If you are like I was as a top leader, I'd find myself writing emails late at night after the kids went to bed, but it didn't look very professional to be emailing someone at 10pm! Schedule it for 8am the next day and know it was taken care of during the time that makes the most sense for you. Another feature of Boomerang is that when you open an email but can't handle it right then, you can "boomerang" it to pop back up to the top of your inbox at a set time. This will happen a lot: Someone emails you a question but you are busy working on something else and you just leave it to deal with later. Rather than risk forgetting about it, or having it get lost among all the other emails in your inbox, set it to pop back up later in the afternoon or at whatever time you know you will be back to answer emails. Using this feature allows me to be much more efficient and intentional with my email time.

The Chrome extension for Gmail called Streak is another great tool for leaders. It is essentially a sales funnel tool or a CRM (Customer Relations Manager) tool. It allows you to take email communication from prospects and put them into "boxes." Then you can set up a sequence for follow-up such as first contact, first follow-up, pending, closing, etc. Though not specifically set up for sponsoring, the "sales" funnel we go through is similar. Within the Streak extension there is also the ability to see when someone has viewed your email, which also makes following up easier and more timely. It also, like Boomerang, has the ability to schedule emails out in advance as well.

The last email tool I will mention is Unroll.me. This is an application that allows you to collect all of your email subscriptions into one email a day so that your inbox is not flooded with advertisements or newsletters. You can choose which subscriptions to "roll up" and which to keep in your inbox. It also lets you easily unsubscribe to those that are no longer relevant. I love this tool as it helps me avoid inbox overwhelm and allows me to see what is important in my inbox right away.

Are You Duplicable?

Duplication in this business is simply the ability to have others do what you do. Ideally, you will see this in your customers, hostesses, and most importantly, your team. Not being duplicable can hurt your sales, booking and sponsoring if people feel they cannot duplicate what you do.

With customers, it shows up as them being able to use the products without a lot of instruction. They see you demonstrate a product at a home party, on a video or at another demonstration. They purchase that product and attempt to do what you did on their own. If it's simple and easy enough to be successful, they want to buy more. When we complicate our demonstrations by adding embellishments or altering the products or presentation with the general public, we reduce our duplicability.

When it comes to online or offline sales parties, duplicability shows up in both our host coaching and our presentations. Think of your parties as a job interview. Your host and guests are thinking about whether they would like to do your job, or if they would like to "hire" you to do the same party with their own friends. Is your party format simple enough so that anyone could do it? Is it fun enough so that others want to repeat it with their own friends? Do your parties appear to be easy on the host, or are you letting her get complicated with refreshments and entertainment for home parties, or elaborate graphics or videos with online parties? Are you giving away so many prizes that it looks like you will barely break even? Or are you keeping it simple and duplicable for everyone? Not keeping your parties easy, simple and fun, is one way to damage your duplicability and prevent others from booking with you, or thinking about doing what you do.

When you are sponsoring others into the business, and then helping those you sponsor to grow their own businesses, duplicability is perhaps the most important trait we can have as representatives and leaders. Lacking duplicability in this area results in less recruiting, or the impression from your team that they can never be like you. When you conduct business, are you doing so in a way that can be easily repeated by others on your team? Are you working your business in a way that makes them want to do what you do? Or are you complicating things so much that they feel inadequate in comparison?

How You Can Simplify to Ensure Duplication

- Demonstrate and display products in the same state as they are sold from the company.

- If you are in a party plan business, use the host coaching guide provided from the company with every hostess. This is important for both offline and online parties.

- Use company-made materials and graphics so customers and prospects know the work is done for them and they don't get the feeling they need to learn Photoshop to be in business.

- Do not overspend on online advertisements, gifts and incentives, inventory or other extras that give the impression this is an expensive business.

- Read and re-read your manual to stay in touch with the information new team members will be reading when they get started.

- If you do want to do extras that would not be considered duplicable, share them only with experienced customers, hostesses or team members who have already mastered the basics.

- Remember: Simple, easy and fun!

Growing Your Team

Online Opportunity Events

In my first book, I shared how to grow your team in the chapter called Sharing the Business Opportunity. The principles are the same whether you are just starting out, or are a seasoned leader—provide value, and build trust and rapport in all your communication with prospects. As a direct selling leader your team will grow even more quickly when you conduct regular opportunity events online. You may be familiar with the offline version of this type of event where one leader—or several—holds a meeting in town and invites her prospects to attend and possibly invites her team to do the same. These can be quite effective if you already have people who have either been customers who may be ready to take things to the next level, or who have shown an interest in finding a home-based business income opportunity.

Thanks to the technology of social media, we can now recreate these online and they are great! Not only does this give you a way to interact with prospects who are not in your local area, but I have found that, in general, people who may be hesitant to come to a live local meeting, perhaps due to fear of being talked into joining, will attend an online opportunity event because there is a lot less pressure. It just feels like less of a commitment to say you will attend an online event, where you are free to click off or type in "no thanks" without any complications. For this reason you may find that your online opportunity meetings are much more lively and well-attended than the offline version.

Just like the offline version, online opportunity events can be held just for yourself and your own prospects, or if you have team members who are building their own teams, consider holding one for your whole organization, letting everyone invite their own prospects to the event. If you are sharing with others in your company, just make sure that everyone is personally inviting their guests and paying extra attention to them. Ideally each representative or leader has already done the work to build loyal relationships with the people they invite. This way the guests know who their sponsor is and there is no confusion.

Platform Options for Online Events

When I was a field leader, I would hold opportunity events in a webinar room or a private business chat room before webinars came along. These worked well because we were able to give our guests a link to join at a certain date/time and we were all gathered on that site. We would then either use plain text chatting or a combination of live video and chatting to get the conversation started. Today we have many more options and clients have been enjoying using live streaming video or social media events the most.

If you are already using a certain platform for your team training (see the chapter called Online Team Meetings and Rallies), then it might make sense to use the same, or something similar for your opportunity events, simply because you and your team will already be familiar with the technology.

One webinar-style platform that is popular right now is Zoom.us because it allows you to have several video screens online at once, as well as screen sharing or displaying presentation slides. If you have the paid account with the Webinar add-on, you can also have it stream to Facebook Live on your Business Page. An additional service I have had success with is AnyMeeting.com — another webinar/video chat program. Both tools have free accounts with some limitations on how many guests you can have online, and paid accounts with more features and larger attendee limits. Another option is to use a stand-alone live desktop streaming platform such as YouTube Live, UStream, or LiveStream or a mobile video streaming app such as Periscope.

One of the most popular and successful ways to conduct online opportunity events is by using a combination of Facebook posts and Facebook Live's video streaming within a Facebook Business Page event. Using Facebook for your opportunity events can make a lot of sense since most of your prospects are probably already using Facebook for social reasons, and the activity you generate on your page by conducting the event will help boost your page's visibility in general. If you are not comfortable yet with live streaming video (see the chapter entitled, Video for Marketing and Training for more tips) you can still hold a very successful opportunity event by simply posting text questions or pictures, or pre-recorded video, similarly to how I recommended conducting Facebook Parties in my first book, *Social Media for Direct Selling Representatives*. Learn more about Facebook Events here: events.facebook.com.

Other social media sites, such as Instagram, can also be used, if you know that your audience prefers them. You could conduct an opportunity event on an Instagram business account set up specifically for this reason, even incorporating Instagram Live, or use a secret Pinterest board. Some people have had success conducting a "Tweet Chat" using a dedicated hashtag they create and then conducting the conversation through a site such as Twubs or TweetGrid or in the Twitter feed itself.

Whatever social media site you use, the concept and agenda would be the same. You meet at a certain time and place online for up to an hour and a half. The only difference would be that, if you are using live video, some of the content would involve you appearing on video asking the questions or interacting with the audience. If you are not using video, the questions and conversations would happen within the posts and comments on each post.

Prepare and Invite

I recommend that you and your team personally invite people to attend your opportunity event, in the way I suggested hosts personally event people to social media parties in my first book. This might mean inviting them by phone or text, or sending a private message or email. The more you can personalize your invitation to each person, the more likely they are to feel special and know you are truly interested in their needs. I would avoid mass invitations because they do not feel as genuine and are less likely to result in attendance. If you are using a social media platform, I recommend inviting in some other way first and getting a "Yes" or "Maybe" before using the built-in "Invite" button. A printed reminder card is a nice touch as well if you have the guests' contact information as a customer or prior host. The more you can connect with potential guests in a way that shows you care, the more likely they are to show up and then sign up!

Once you have a "Yes" or "Maybe" then offer specific instructions on how they can access the meeting and what to expect as far as timing. You can also share the link or instructions to your main social media networks, or by email or other methods to your general network. You never know who may be ready to hear more but simply hasn't given you the "green flags" yet! Publicize the event whenever you can. In the case of online opportunity events, the more the merrier!

You might also invite everyone on your team to attend, even if they do not have prospects who are attending. This way they get to participate in the conversation and get excited about their business all over again, too!

Online Opportunity Event Agenda

The agenda I use is inspired by an idea I learned and used for offline opportunity meetings in my local area, and then adapted for online use thanks to one of my former business coaches, Jane Deuber, years ago. She graciously allowed me to share the concept here. She calls it "An Evening of Exploration."

If you are doing a multi-consultant event, invite some of your leaders to take on different parts, such as coming up with verbiage and graphics for each question and posting to the event. Be sure all of your representatives know how important it is to engage in the comments of each post. This will increase the sense of community among guests and consultants. The more comments there are the more fun it is for everyone.

1. Welcome everyone, write down attendance and have everyone share the answer to a "get to know you" question, such as where they are from and what they are most excited

about with this company. All participants do this— representatives as well as your guests.

2. Share a brief synopsis of the company history and its mission. You might want to also add a question to encourage comments such as, "Which part of this resonates with you the most?"

3. Explain that together, you will be discussing a series of questions in which you encourage them to share answers with the group, but if they aren't comfortable doing that, they can simply write them down for later reflection.

4. Introduce the Evening of Exploration Questions one by one. Through these questions you will facilitate a discussion about their needs and desires regarding joining this business, emphasizing that these questions will help them discover whether this is the business that could be the answer for them. There is no pressure, but the goal is to be informed. The sharing in this section can be very touching!

5. Give them time to reflect on each of the following Exploration Questions and possibly write down or post the answers. You may not get to all of them! If posting on a social media event, it is a good idea to number the questions and create a graphic to represent each one.

   ▪ Question 1: What do you love most about your life right now?

   ▪ Question 2: What is important to you at this stage of your life?

   ▪ Question 3: What motivated you to come this evening?

- Question 4: If you could wave a magic wand and change one thing in your life right now, what would it be?

- Question 5: Is there anything else you would change?

- Question 6: What would that feel like to have that be your reality?

- Question 7: If you could choose one thing in your life that could be different one year from now, and you *knew* you could not fail, what would you want to be different?

- Question 8: Are you willing to try something new that could bring about these positive changes in your life?

- Question 9: Would you be open to seeing how this business opportunity could impact your life in the coming year?

6. Share what you personally enjoy most about your business — your "Why." Invite your current representatives to share as well. Have those who are already in the business tell the group what they love most about it, or what benefits being in the business has given them or their family. Try having them share a video directly to the event, or share a link to their pre-recorded "Why Story" video if they have one. This adds a more personal element.

7. Open Question/Answer period. Ask your guests what their burning questions or curiosities are so that the group can help them understand — anything goes! Encourage current distributors to chime in with answers as well.

8. Ask the audience, on a scale of 1 to 10, 10 being "Sign me up right now!" and 1 being "Get me out of here!" how are they

feeling about this company being something they would like to join? Explore in the comments possibilities of what would bring them closer to a 10, or give them instructions on how to sign up! Set a follow-up phone call within 48 hours.

9. Conduct a door prize drawing by either using an existing contact form, or by setting up a Google Form for free online, where you collect contact information. When you receive the entries by email, you can choose a random winner. On your form you might want to ask them questions such as what their Scale of 1-10 number was, or ask what they are most excited about or any questions they still have. Be sure to also include a space for them to tell you who invited them to the event, so that you can forward the information to the right person. Using these forms makes follow up so easy!

10. Offer a special gift for anyone who signs up within a certain time frame. For example you might want to offer 10 catalogs when someone signs up by the end of the weekend, so they can get started sharing about their new business while they wait for materials from the company.

11. Thank everyone for attending and make sure they know how to get ahold of you or research more information on your replicated website.

12. Be sure you and your team members who brought prospects FOLLOW UP! Most new consultants will commit after the event during your follow-up, not right on the spot during the event.

The Pillow Test

This is another great idea from Jane Deuber that works offline or online. When someone really can't commit yet, but they are somewhat interested, have them try the pillow test. Maybe they have doubts about being able to do the business, or about the cost of the starter kit. Maybe they would like to talk it over with their husband first. Through a private message or to the group as a whole, post something like, "Do you want to give it the pillow test? What this means is that you leave this event and tonight when you go to bed, try not to think of a single thing about the opportunity. Put it out of your mind completely. If at some point during the night or the next morning, you find that thoughts of starting this business keep creeping into your mind, it might be that this really is something you should seriously consider! I'll be following up _____ (tomorrow at a certain time) to find out how it went. Does that sound like a deal?" If this was posted in a public post, ask who would like to commit to trying the pillow test—they can comment "ME!"

Just be sure you or their sponsor do follow-up the next day! I've found that using the Pillow Test allows your guests to save face if they are not quite ready to commit, and they can consider all the options after the event. In most cases, they can't stop thinking about it, and allowing them this space to really reflect on their own actually gets them even more excited!

LinkedIn for Leaders

inkedIn is a powerful networking tool, especially for a leader who is seeking new team members. LinkedIn was originally designed to be used for job seekers to be able to post their resumé online and find a job. LinkedIn has evolved over the years to also include 1) networking among business owners who offer and receive referrals, 2) posting status updates to the general news feed that show up for your connections 3) writing and sharing longer blog-style articles, and 4) interacting in professional discussion groups.

For those of us in direct sales, the opportunity with LinkedIn is to position ourselves as experts in developing and succeeding in a home-based business. This will help you attract new people to your team. Occasionally you will find that people become curious about your product when they first meet you on LinkedIn, but more often you will find LinkedIn most useful for team building.

If you have decided to more seriously focus on using LinkedIn to grow your team, I recommend adding the following tasks to your daily and weekly social media schedule for best results. For the general direct seller, it is not necessary to interact as frequently on LinkedIn. However, if you really want to leverage its power as a leader, consistent activity is key.

Update Something in Your Profile Once or Twice Each Month

- Change the wording in any of the paragraphs to more closely align with your topic, expertise or particular type of business.

- Add media to your summary or experience sections such as a video, a PDF, or a captivating image.

- Check and improve the wording of your titles, headlines or skills. This brings attention to your profile.

Comment on or Like Three to Five Status Updates in the News Feed, Ideally Every Day

- From the home page, scroll through to see the status updates your connections have posted.

- Make relevant comments when you can, click "like" or share their post with your own network as a new status update.

- Zero in on prospects and interact with them more than others throughout the month.

Post a New Status Update on Your Personal Profile Daily

- Be sure to post mostly non-promotional, helpful, useful or relevant content, educational tips, ideas, articles or updates on your business. Be aware that LinkedIn is very different from Facebook. Your family or pet pictures, recipes or funny videos do not belong on LinkedIn.

- Share links to interesting articles, blog posts or news items that your network would appreciate, and bring the expertise back to yourself by adding a thoughtful caption.

- Minimize blatant marketing messages on your status updates. Once in a while is okay but the vast majority of your posts should be non-promotional in order to build trust with your connections.

Write and Publish a Long-Form Article Once, Twice or More Per Month

- Articles on LinkedIn are like blog posts. 350 words or more are best in order to provide value.

- Refrain from pitching in your articles. These should be informative and useful whether or not one does business with you. Possible topics might be about working from home, leadership, business issues, or a subject related to but not directly about your product. The idea here is to establish your expertise and also to have your article show up in searches.

- Include a separator line at the end of your article and then a short bio or byline explaining who you are and how someone could get ahold of you (including a link to your website!)

Connect to Interesting New People Each Week

- Use People You May Know from the home page to find common connections that may be of interest. Find this under the My Network tab or at <u>linkedin /people/pymk.</u>

- You might also try the Advanced Search where you can sort people based on location or different keywords they may have in their profiles.

- Always include a personal note indicating why you are connecting, such as mentioning something you have in common.

Recommend One to Two People Per Month

- LinkedIn Recommendations are for people you have hired or worked with directly and include written testimonials about them, as opposed to Endorsements, which aren't as powerful.

- Offer a sincere recommendation based on a specific job, event or project whenever appropriate.

- Only recommend those you would recommend otherwise — not out of obligation. Sometimes the recommendation is reciprocated, but is not to be expected.

Request One to Two Recommendations Per Month

- When finalizing something like a home party or demonstration with a host, or perhaps after completing a vendor booth obligation, request a recommendation from the person you worked with or reported to within 48 hours. Do this by clicking on the three small dots near the name on the profile of the person from whom you are requesting the recommendation.

- You must already be connected on LinkedIn in order to request a recommendation from someone.

- In the request, gently remind the person of any verbal feedback you may have gotten from them, or privately message this information to help them remember the quality of your work.

Comment on Three to Five Posts Within Targeted LinkedIn Groups Per Week

- Use the Search feature to sort by Groups to find discussion groups your network is using or about a topic your target prospect might be interested in. Type a word into the search such as "direct sales" and click the magnifying glass to get the full results. Then click on Groups. See below for some LinkedIn Group suggestions.

- Your thoughtful comments to popular posts demonstrate your expertise and increase your visibility.

- Adjust your Group Settings to control email notifications if you like.

Post Relevant Questions, Tips, Links to Blog Posts or Articles in Targeted Groups One to Three Times Per Week

- Spark thoughtful discussions about issues, concerns, news or simply questions you have that are relevant to that particular group. Group members enjoy demonstrating their own expertise in response to questions posted.

- When you have a new LinkedIn article yourself, add a link to it to the group, with an introductory caption.

- When you come across outside articles or blog posts that you feel the group members would appreciate, share them as well, adding your own comments and perhaps a discussion question.

- Most LinkedIn Groups are pitch-free zones. Again, your goal is to establish your expertise and perhaps be a resource to others who then may seek out more information or refer others to you.

Finding Relevant Groups

Following is a list of LinkedIn Groups that, as of this publication date, are actively allowing direct sellers to network and either post about their opportunities or start discussions that may help establish you as an expert leader. There are a variety of groups geared toward either the party plan model, or network marketing, or MLM but do not let that concern you. Even if you consider your business network marketing vs. party plan or you do not care for the MLM model, you are still welcome to participate in any of these. The truth is, people will often be involved in one type of direct selling but when they are between companies, or perhaps they have been away from the industry awhile and want to come back, they would appreciate learning about something new. I've listed them starting with the largest groups which will lead to the greatest exposure for you.

MLM Pros
linkedin.com/groups/86576/profile

The Art of Network Marketing
linkedin.com/groups/985927

MLM Network
linkedin.com/groups/119830

I Work From Home
linkedin.com/groups/1816746

Multi-Level Marketing Group (MLM)
linkedin.com/groups/133858

DSWA — The Alliance
linkedin.com/groups/118223

Network Marketing — News, Events & Success Tips
linkedin.com/groups/3820056/profile

Building Network Marketing — MLM
linkedin.com/groups/819287/profile

Global Home-Based Business
linkedin.com/groups/2876320

Business Opportunity Seekers
linkedin.com/groups/2311823

MLM & Network Marketing 2011
linkedin.com/groups/3568751/profile

Direct Sales Club
linkedin.com/groups/1987572/profile

Power4--MLM and Network Marketing
linkedin.com/groups/2127575/profile

Network Marketers Group
linkedin.com/groups/1477707/profile

The World of Direct Selling
linkedin.com/groups/1941286

Success From Home Fans
linkedin.com/groups/52921/profile
Network Marketing Pro
linkedin.com/groups/5108077/profile

Party Plan Companies Networking Club
linkedin.com/groups/4430134

Multi-Level Marketing (MLM) Entrepreneurs
linkedin.com/groups/2416432/profile

Free Network Marketing Help
linkedin.com/groups/3876437/profile

MLM Leaders Directory
linkedin.com/groups/3154049/profile

Welcome To MLM
linkedin.com/groups/4860551/profile

Direct Sales Opportunities
linkedin.com/groups/4786143/profile

Home Party Plans Monthly Specials
linkedin.com/groups/2890288/profile

If you are looking to build a professional team this year, LinkedIn is the place to be. Those who are looking for work, or to add income to an existing job, are exploring opportunities there, so being visible and helpful on LinkedIn will pay off!

Hashtags for Direct Selling

Have you been using hashtags on your social media posts? Finding the right keywords to use — and those that are active enough to attract new people to your network — can be a challenge. Here's a starter list you might want to try. Hashtags work best on Instagram and Twitter, and with limited success on the other platforms. Experiment for yourself. Add two to five hashtags when appropriate, and people who are interested in the topics might find your post and interact with you and your business!

I like to use them at the end of the posts, kind of like category tags, vs. embedded within the text, as those are awkward and hard to read — and can confuse some people! The social networks that use hashtags the most are Instagram, Twitter and Google+, although they are taking off on Facebook and Pinterest as well.

Using a hashtag gives your post exposure to people searching on those words or hashtags. For example if someone reads a post about makeup on a popular women's magazine's Instagram account that has the hashtag #makeup or #cosmetics, they can click on those hashtag words and find other posts (like yours!) where the user also included those hashtags.

In this way, you can get exposure to other brands' networks and get discovered by more people. Some social media users also use the search boxes extensively when looking for information about certain topics. Hashtags also come up in the search results as they are considered popular, or trending, topics.

Direct Sales in General
#dstips
#directsales
#partyplan
#directselling
#networkmarketing
#mlm

Business Opportunity
#bizopp
#incomeopportunity
#businessopportunity

Women/Moms in Business
#wahm (work at home mom)
#mompreneur
#sahm (stay at home mom)
#womenbiz
#mombiz

General Business/Home Business
#homebiz
#smallbiztips

#biztips
#bizitalk
#entrepreneur

These are the more general hashtags. I'm sure you will be able to think of and explore others that are specific to your product, service or industry. For example, a jewelry company might want to use #jewelry #bling #accessories or a cookware company might use #cooking #recipe #kitchen.

A great tool I love for discovering hashtags about a specific topic is Hashtagify.me. Type in a general keyword and you'll get other related hashtags. The objective is to attract interested leads, not others who are marketing their own businesses — or worse, spammers — which can be a challenge.

Build a Local Team

According to Google, 97 percent of people who frequent local businesses find them through the Internet first. That figure is staggering to me and shows it doesn't really make a lot of sense to ignore Internet marketing. By being visible on the Internet, you stand a good chance of attracting business locally in your area.

What can you do to reach out online to local people in your own backyard? It used to be that consumers consulted a large printed book of yellow pages when they needed to find a photographer, bookkeeper or realtor. If they weren't sure where to go for art supplies, books or pizza, they let their fingers do the walking. The vast majority of today's consumers — locally and globally — turn to online searches and Internet directories to find what they are looking for. Within a few seconds they are given information about the closest service provider, restaurant or shop, along with real time customer reviews, ratings and "buzz" that influences their decision on which business to patronize.

Making sure that your business shows up in the results for local searches is determined by whether or not you have your town, city, county or region listed on your website, blog, or social media profiles, as well as if you have a presence on several of the social networks online that are geared toward serving a local clientele. The following resources will get you started in creating more local doorways into your business.

Even though you more than likely do not have a physical storefront where you do business, you can still get listed as if you did. This will help people who are looking for local support or a local opportunity to be able to find you. Internet marketing is great for expanding your business all over your country or even the world, but nothing beats having a local team that with whom you can meet in person and conduct live meetings and training events. Following are some ways to get found locally.

Interact with Local Connections

One of the easiest ways to attract local business is to interact a little more with local online connections and businesses. You can sort your local Facebook friends into a "Friend List" that you set up specifically for this reason. Facebook will automatically create a "smart list" for people in and around the location you list as your home town, but you may need to set up another for a broader reach. For example, I live in the town of Rohnert Park but I have a Friend List I created for Sonoma County, which expands out further, and I have another Friend List for San Francisco Bay Area that goes out even further. I also have Friend Lists for Southern California and the Sacramento area. Creating these lists helps me interact more with people in those areas when I am promoting something in their area such as a speaking engagement. Or, when I post something new I can set my post to go out specifically to people on those lists.

Twitter has its own version of these lists called simply Twitter Lists. You can easily sort your connections into a locally named list, such as Northern California for me, and when you check on that list's news feed, it is easier to interact with people on those lists. On LinkedIn you can also add a tag to your contacts and when you use LinkedIn's search you can more easily find people you've tagged by location.

See my chapter on <u>Social Media Time Savers</u> for more information about these geographic lists.

List Your Business in Online Directories

Yelp is the most popular business rating, feedback and referral social network. Because of its popularity, when your business is listed, your listing will have a powerful presence on the web. Past customers can write reviews and testimonials on your business profile, and potential new customers can find you, learn more about your business, and contact you. The community of Yelp users is expansive and social, and connections are readily exposed to their friends' favorite businesses. Since Yelp users are directed to businesses closest to their chosen metropolitan area, local people are drawn to you and share your information with other local people. When filling out a business owner profile on Yelp, be sure to thoroughly describe yourself, your business and your company mission, and include all of the extras such as photos of your product or service in action, and any special offers or announcements. You will have the opportunity to make sure your physical location is unlisted, since your business is home-based and technically "mobile" i.e. you go to where your customers and prospects are or meet them in public locations.

The Merchant Circle network is a stand-alone online community geared toward connecting local independent businesses with their neighbors. Their platform allows businesses to create mini-websites, blogs, coupons and newsletters—free. Consumers who prefer to use local business instead of chain stores or franchises appreciate being able to depend on Merchant Circle to steer them toward truly local, responsive companies and service providers who offer them incentives to do business with them. Emails to your local neighborhood go out on a regular basis from the Merchant Circle network, and your business information is included. Even if you do not have a website of your own or a blog already, creating a presence on Merchant Circle is another powerful way to engage with your local community and establish your presence as "the" local representative or leader.

Meetup is another way to get additional local and online exposure, as well as being very highly indexed by search engines. When you join Meetup as a member, you can browse any number of topics and find local gatherings to join for networking or to learn something new. Some meetings are weekly and some are monthly. Some are just for special interests, and some are business-oriented. When you join an established Meetup, you will be able to create a bio or profile that can be linked to your business information and website. This profile, and any activity within the Meetup page, is also visible to outside search engines. Be sure to include the fact that you are looking for more people to join your team and start their own careers with your company. To get even more visibility, consider organizing your own Meetup (for a fee) or list a current group or workshop you conduct via Meetup's system. If you are holding regular public meetings, shows or opportunity events, it might be worthwhile to get them listed on Meetup, since you will be piggybacking on the site's reach.

NextDoor is a newer platform that many people are enjoying as a way to connect to others in their actual neighborhood within their cities or towns. There are forums and classified advertisements, community events and government announcements, as well as people just looking to connect with each other and be "neighborly." As a business, you are allowed to create a business account with limited functionality at this time. Businesses cannot interact with people in the neighborhood, but members may comment on the business, find and contact you from within the site, and recommend you as a business or service provider. For this reason, I do recommend creating a business account and you can do so at nextdoor.com/business. Like me, though, you might find that the conversations and personal relationships you can develop using a personal account to be beneficial as well. You can have both.

Google, Yahoo and Bing Local Business Listings

Each of the three major search engines have local business listings where you can create a complete profile that outlines your business description, location, web addresses, categories and photos. Take the time to submit your home-based business listing to Yahoo, Google and Bing LOCAL.

- yext.com (for Yahoo)

- google.com/business

- bingplaces.com

Once you do, customers can rate your service, leave a review or testimonial, and share your profile with their contacts. This is a great place to emphasize your business opportunity and leadership, informing people that you offer your company's products. Creating a local account on the search engines requires verification by phone or mail and that adds credibility to each of the listings, since people know that the businesses listed are verified to be who they say they are. Since these directories are associated with each search engine, having a presence there means that your listing is bumped to the top of search results when someone in your area uses the search engine to find someone who does what you do. Do not worry about having to list your address, since you will be able to mark it as invisible once your listing is complete.

Locally-Based Social Media Groups

Most major social media platforms have a local component to them. There are Facebook Groups and LinkedIn Groups about your local community or nearest metropolitan area. Twitter has hashtags that you can follow and use on your posts, and Pinterest has boards people have created about their local area. Use the search function in any of these platforms by typing in your location names to find groups that are already discussing local issues, or sharing tips and ideas about a specific city or region. Jump into the conversation and share your own ideas, and you will start to connect with new people who share that interest. If there isn't already a group for your local area, consider starting one yourself and you will attract others who like to network locally online.

Generate Interest with Instagram Contests

Contests on Instagram are a great way to achieve goals such as increasing engagement, getting new followers, sending people to your website, and introducing people to your opportunity.

Instagram contests have guidelines similar to those on Facebook, which you may have read about in *Social Media for Direct Selling Representatives*.

Promotions on Instagram must include the following:

- A complete release of Instagram by each entrant or participant.

- Acknowledgement that the promotion is in no way sponsored, endorsed or administered by, or associated with, Instagram.

As always, please be sure your contest is in compliance with your company policies and state regulations regarding sweepstakes. Make sure the instructions are clear in your caption, such as how to win, if they can enter more than once and if there are any age or other eligibility requirements. Be sure to add the hashtag #contest! It will help you attract even more entrants!

An example of the verbiage to add to your contest might be:

This contest is open to anyone 18 and over in the United States. One entry per person. Winner will be announced on this post and through private message on ABC Date. This contest is in no way sponsored, endorsed or administered by, or associated with, Instagram and by entering this contest you hereby agree to release Instagram of any liability.

Here are some ideas that seem to work well on Instagram:

- Announce a giveaway that will be randomly drawn from anyone who comments on your picture.

- Give something away to the very last commenter at a specific time.

- Ask your followers to post pictures with specific content—such as them holding your product, or a video saying why they want to win—and to use a certain hashtag to label the picture, or to tag your account in the comments or caption so you are notified. Then choose a winner randomly.

- Have a photo contest where you will judge a photo (identified by tagging you or with a hashtag) based on certain criteria. Could be most creative, or best use of filters, most inspiring caption etc. You be the judge or as part of the contest, ask your viewers to like the picture they want to win and the picture with the most likes gets the prize.

- Run a scavenger hunt contest. In your post list three or more items your viewers need to take pictures of and post with your tag/hashtag. Once they complete all of the items, they will be entered into the contest. At the end, you will randomly draw a winner from all of the completed entries. Be as simple or crazy as you think your audience can handle!

- Play a guessing game. Take a picture of you or your product in a location others would know, or doing something they can guess. Have them guess your location or activity and choose a winner among those who answered correctly.

- Have a seasonal/holiday photo contest. Have your readers dress up or decorate for a specific holiday, and post something specific in the caption with your unique hashtag. Choose among the participants.

- Ask your followers to be creative by posting a photo that depicts something specific. For example, if Valentine's Day is coming, post a picture that represents true love and use hashtag #trueloveKC (the KC to identify it as Karen Clark's vs. random people using the #truelove tag!)

- Simply announce that all _____ (some activity such as new subscribers to your newsletter or comments on your Facebook post) within a certain time period will be entered to win, and to check your bio for the link to the specific action you want them to take.

- Finish your sentence—Have readers fill in the blanks of a sentence such as the last three words of a song lyric, or three favorite colors, or I want to win because... You can require a set answer or any answer in order to enter the contest..

- People love to play to win and the prize value isn't as important as is an engaging topic that will encourage comments and likes. Getting lots of comments will help your community get to know each other and get excited about your business. It will also help increase your visibility on Instagram as your post will seem to be "popular" and be more likely to show up in the Discover tab. As a leader, customize your contests to focus on information or sharing that has to do with your business opportunity, working from home, financial freedom and other topics that might appeal to general audiences so that they can also learn about the business side of things.

Using a Public Team Map

T hanks to a tip from my friend Patrick Schwerdtfeger, author of *Marketing Shortcuts for the Self-Employed*, I've added a Google Map to the bottom of my website's home page. It not only shows where I've been as a social media speaker, but below it, I list those places and also places where I would like to speak. This makes it possible for people who might be looking in the search engines for a direct sales keynote speaker on social media in those areas to find me. How might you use this as a leader?

Why not create a Google Map for your team, so that their locations are listed in case people are searching online for a local representative? This map can be embedded on your team website or blog if you have one, or the link to the map can simply be shared on social media or by email. You can create a map that pinpoints places where you have consultants or team members, and even list places where you are looking to build a team. Do you think this will help people find you when they are looking for your opportunity? I think so! Here's how to set it up:

1. While logged into your Google account, simply go to google.com/maps and on the top left look for the three little lines to access the Google Map Menu.

2. Click on Your Places then Maps and then See All Your Maps.

3. Click the red Create a New Map button.

4. Click on the words Untitled Map and give your new map a name, such as Karen Clark's XYZ Company Independent Director's Team Members, and then a description.

5. Now type in any location in the search bar to find cities and on their pop-up screen you will see the option to Add to Map.

6. When you are done adding cities, click the Share button to create a link you can share out, and on the same screen make the map public.

7. For those with a blog/website, try the following to customize your map so you can embed it on your site:

   - Get the map to appear the way you would like it by moving around or using the +/- buttons to zoom in or out.

   - Click on the three little dots at the top, and click on Embed on My Site. You will see the code to use, and can copy and paste that wherever you would like to display the map. Note that you might want to adjust the size within the code. The default is 640x480, which you can find in the code under height and width.

   - To insert it, visit your website or blog and on the page where you would like to display this map, such as on your Home page, edit the text/HTML to paste the map code into position. If you have a WordPress blog site, look for the button in your page editor that looks like two arrows such as < >. This will allow you to access the HTML code editor. Once you've pasted the code, click it again to go back to the Visual editor.

- Add a paragraph under your map about where you have team members, listing the names of the cities and states. Add some sentences about where you are "now seeking consultants in the cities of..." and name specific metropolitan areas or states.

As I mentioned, you can link to your map and post on your social media sites, especially the public ones (visible to Google) such as your Facebook Business Page. Simply add the names of cities where you are seeking new team members in the caption. You can go further by looking at your map (under My Places) within Google Maps, click on Edit. Change the Privacy and Sharing Setting to Public, and add a meaningful description about your business and perhaps add a text link to where people can find out more. This map will still be "findable" within Google, whether or not you ever post it on a website or to social media. It is exposure for your business!

If you are a leader of a larger organization, there is one more strategy you can take—invite Collaborators to your map. With this, you would be adding permission for other people (maybe other leaders within your organization) to add their **own** locations to your overall organization map. To do this, simply click on My Places and then click on your map name and then click on Collaborate. Type in your leaders' email addresses, and add a little message explaining what this is all about. If you would like them to be able to invite even more people as well, there is a setting for that on the right. In most cases you will want to control who is invited to the map. However, it is up to you and your situation if you would like to make it a large, expansive map.

It is really fun for your team members to see where everyone is located. You could, of course, just use this internally in your team Facebook Group, but I think it's great exposure to keep it public as well. Something else that might be fun would be to run a contest for your team to see if you can have a consultant in every state or province. List all the areas where you have someone and all the areas where you still need consultants. I know of a leader who also used a Google map to list parties booked by her team. She would then run a contest to see which state had the most parties booked over a certain time, such as January, and all the consultants in the "winning" state got recognition for being so active. You can really get creative with this, whether you keep the map public or create some private ones. There is no limit to how many of these live interactive maps you create.

When a Company Closes

As an experienced direct seller, you have more than likely seen some companies come and some companies go. Over time you will find this is a normal part of the cycle in this industry. However, each time it happens many of us in the industry are nonetheless deeply saddened. When a company closes, it is almost like a death in the family, even for those of us not directly involved in the company. Like a death, it reminds us of our mortality and makes everyone think — could it happen to me, too? The reality is your business, your livelihood, and the lifestyle that goes along with it, are at the mercy of the company thriving over time.

One of the worst things to watch when a company closes are the predators who swoop in to recruit the grieving representatives over to their own opportunity, not out of the goodness of their hearts but out of greed and selfishness. When I was growing up I was taught that one should never profit from another's misfortune. When you see someone suffering, you extend a hand in service and lift them up. You don't push them down further, or ask them to do something for YOU.

If you are building your online presence correctly, you have many doorways into your business and you have connections to people who know you, like you and trust you. If you come from service and integrity in your business, the right people will find you when the time is right for them. Perhaps they already have considered your opportunity as their Plan B because they have admired you and how you conduct yourself online. Or they have watched what a difference your product or opportunity has made for you and your family.

Be there for them. Answer any questions they may have, but do not swoop in with messages about how awesome your compensation plan is, or with a special offer they will receive from you if they join your company, or how blessed you are to be with a company who doesn't have X, Y, or Z issues like theirs did.

- Are you findable in social media? If someone were to search for your opportunity in their area, can they find you?

- Do you have a presence in the places where people might be going when they want to research new opportunities?

- Does your online presence speak to your personality, your leadership and your desire to teach and inspire others?

- Or are your social accounts only a reflection of what you hope to get, not to give?

- Does your social media presence make me want to do business with you, to join your team, to make your direct selling company my new family?

When consultants from various direct selling companies act like vultures swooping in on fresh meat, it hurts the representatives from the company that is closing, and it damages the reputation of our industry since it is done so publicly through social media. Give the consultants time to grieve and those who are ready to find you, will.

On the other side of things, starting a new direct selling business after your company has closed requires doing a lot of research, as well as learning to trust again. It is essential to build rapport with the right leader, since you will be taking a giant leap of faith. Make sure you are there for those on your team who need you to lift them up in support.

Training and Supporting Your Team

Facebook Groups for Your Team

Many direct selling leaders have found success in training, supporting and recognizing their teams using Facebook Groups. This is a convenient way to connect your team members to each other — and to you! Using a Facebook Group (or two or three…) will help you develop and sustain a sense of community among your team in a way that is hard to beat. Even if you have a local team and conduct in-person meetings and special events, you will still benefit from having a private social media forum to keep the excitement going and foster friendships among your team. In fact, you might even find that some of the introverts on your team tend to open up a lot more using the Facebook Group, so it is especially important for them to have such a place to go. You can also use your Facebook Groups as a way to remind your team of any trainings, meetings or incentives you or the company offer. Since most people are on Facebook several times a day, why not provide support and training there? You are much more likely to get participation if you literally meet people where they are.

There are many built-in features you can use with a Facebook Group such as the Files tab where you can store important documents, training handouts or marketing materials. The Photos tab allows you to create albums or organize any images you share for trainings, and you can use the Events tab to remind your team of both online and offline events. If you have a smaller group (less than 250 members) you can also conduct a group chat. Your team will really appreciate the ability to search within your group using the search bar, too. Although I do not recommend Facebook Groups for outright selling (this is a Facebook Jail issue as outlined in my first book), they are ideal for sharing support and information.

Most leaders set up one group for their whole team and feel pretty satisfied doing it that way. However, as you become more proficient using your group more for training and even coaching, or as your team grows into a larger organization you may want to consider setting up more than one. For example, it is a great idea to set up a Team Resources group specifically for you to share files and images organized in albums, or to post links to articles on your team blog if you have one. Think of the Resources group as a sort of archive or library your team can access at any time, and to which you can post new items you either create yourself or share from another source, without worrying about filling the main group feed with multiple posts.

Another secondary group might be a Team Social group. This is where your team members can go simply for social topics or "off topic" conversations that aren't business-related. They can share about their families or hobbies without distracting people from the main focus of your team group. In this group you might want to have a question of the week that gets conversations going, or assign that job to another leader on your team. When done correctly, a Team Social group is very effective at building a culture of positivity and support. When they meet up at your next conference they will already feel like they know each other personally and no one will feel alone.

As your team grows, I also recommend you create separate groups for new consultants and new leaders, and possibly one for your top leaders if you have a large organization with multiple directors who are building their own organizations. Although it may be intimidating to think about how you will manage separate groups like this, I would suggest you think about having some of your leaders share the responsibilities (after all, their team members are in the groups, too) or decide on a day of the week to post in them. Unlike your public-facing marketing pages, these specialized groups do not need daily support. For example, you might set up a task each week or a challenge, and then at the end of the week, check in to see how everyone did.

Although Facebook does not have a built-in post scheduler for Facebook Groups, it is very easy to set up scheduled or recurring posts through outside applications such as CinchShare, which will post to groups. Ideally, your team will have notifications set to "on for all posts" and be manually checking the group each day or each week (train them to do this!). Therefore, there is no risk of using a scheduler affecting the visibility of your posts. See my chapter on <u>Social Media Time Savers</u> for more information.

In your main group, remember you are always modeling for your team, so it is okay to not post every day. However, your goal should be to stay active and available throughout the week if possible. If you like the idea of daily posts, consider an "editorial calendar" to start and keep conversations going. For example: Monday Motivation, Tuesday Tips/Training, Wednesday Weekly News/Announcements, Thursday Team How-to, and Fun Friday. I do not recommend posting in your team group more than two or three times a day for the same reasons I do not recommend that for your marketing posts: People start to get overwhelmed and will tune you out! Post once a day, but pack it with a punch! If you have more than one image to share, do it in a multiple image post, or create an album for that topic and post the album to the group.

Some leaders set up weekly trainings much like you would an opportunity event as described in the <u>Online Opportunity Events</u> chapter of this book. For those, you would create an Event within your group and post videos, images, links and text to elaborate on a training topic at a certain time on a certain day. These would then remain on your Events tab, and all group members are automatically invited and receive notifications. It is a nice way to keep your trainings organized, and you can always send the link to a past training to a newer consultant or leader who may have missed it.

Steps to Setting Up a Facebook Group

1. On the desktop version of Facebook, go to <u>groups.fb.com</u> and click Create Group. I recommend using the desktop because the mobile apps do not have all the group setup features.

2. Give your group a title using your team name. Be sure to follow company guidelines when naming your Group. Example: Karen's Rising Stars vs. using the company name.

3. Add one trusted person to the group so it will let you start (you can remove them later if needed.)

4. Choose Closed group as the privacy setting. (Secret is another option but you will need to be friends with each person and manually add them for that to work, vs. giving

all team members the link to join and then approving them, or inviting them by email.)

5. Choose an icon identifier on the following panel.

6. Add a group cover image, This can be something generic and seasonal, or you can create a graphic with important information each month, or consider highlighting team members for recognition, etc. It can be changed any time and the group receives a notification when you update it.

7. Click the small > on the top right to access your group info and then click on edit group settings.

8. Choose the Group Type such as Support, Team or Custom. This setting does not matter so much for a private group, but it is a way to let new members know what the group is about before they join. Do not use the Buy/Sell group option. This is designed for those in your community who are selling used items to each other — not for business.

9. Change Membership Approval to "require an admin to approve." This will prevent your team from accidentally adding their friends to the group without vetting them as team members.

10. On the desktop version of Facebook you can set up a Group Address that will become your team's group URL as well. For example: facebook.com/groups/karensrisingstars. This should ideally coordinate with the group title. This gives you a shorter link to send to your new team members so they can join the group, and it also allows you to email your posts to the group, which is a lesser-used feature but could come in handy.

11. Fill out your group description. Include information about your business (since it may be seen by non-members) and any posting guidelines. It is a good idea to set standards for your group that includes requiring them to stay positive and discuss anything that is specific to their own personal situation with you or customer service. This way you can prevent negativity from infecting your team! It can be edited any time. For example:

This is a private group for Independent ABC Representatives and is by invitation only. If you have found this group and are not yet a Representative, please visit mywebsite.com to get more information. Group Member Guidelines: This group is intended for positive support and interaction among members of Karen Clark's team of Independent ABC Representatives. Please feel free to use this group as a resource for your business and as a way to communicate with me and your fellow representatives. In the spirit of our company's vision and mission, please keep all conversations informative, supportive and positive, as well as relevant to the entire group. If you have a particular personal challenge, please bring that up privately. Please also refrain from promoting or discussing any other product, event or opportunity unrelated to ABC Company. Finally, please bring up any customer service issues with the company directly by contacting custserv@abcompany.com.

12. Post anything interesting you'd like them to see when they arrive—information, pictures, files, etc.

13. Email or message the group URL to your team to invite them to join. This is recommended vs. using the +Add People. This way they have the option to join it themselves, and only when they are ready. Otherwise, they will begin getting email notifications and may get confused. You can also

use the Invite by Email option on the right. This will send them an email from Facebook letting them know you have invited them to the group and they can then click the link to join.

14. Approve your new members as they come on board. If you have a large team, you may want to ask for some help with this, or make some of your leaders admins on the page (in addition to you) so they can approve their own team members.

15. Explain how to set their notifications to See All Posts so they do not miss a thing, and tell them to check the group manually every day anyway in case they miss a notification.

Using the Files Tab

Facebook provides within Groups only, a place to store Files. You can either create a "Doc" within the Files area (a new document), or you can upload your own files to be stored there. This can be useful for new consultant training, company fliers, or other approved marketing pieces to which you want your team to have access. Files accepted are plain text documents, Word/Excel/Office documents and PDFs. Use the Photos section to upload images or screen captures to albums you name based on topic.

Other Features to Try

▪ If you find someone posts something negative, salesy or otherwise unwelcome, do *not* click on the upper right of the post to Hide it—that only hides it from *you*. It does not delete the post from the group—others can still see it. To remove it from everyone's view, you must click Delete. I recommend you take a screen shot of it first for your records and then privately message the person to lovingly explain that you are deleting it because it is not in alignment with your group guidelines.

- You can "Pin" important posts to the very top of the Group. You can only pin one post at a time. For example: the training schedule or this week's focus—but it can easily be unpinned and changed. This makes it easier to highlight something important that will stay at the top instead of losing it as new posts are posted. One disadvantage to this is that people viewing the group on mobile devices will see a small line that says "View pinned post" instead of the actual post and need to click that line to view it.

- I mentioned using Albums to organize your training. In the desktop version of your Facebook Group find Albums in your Photos tab. If you have set them up by topic in advance as mentioned in the <u>Social Media Time Savers</u> chapter, your group can become a robust resource for your team.

- Setting up a Facebook Event within your team group is a great way to make sure your members will receive reminders about any team meetings or calls or company trainings or conferences. You can use it simply as a way to gather RSVPs and remind people about the events, or you can use the event page itself as a way to carry on conversations around the event—such as generating excitement prior to the event, sharing pictures from the event, or following up with discussion about the posted topics. As I mentioned earlier, you can also use the group event page as a place to conduct trainings, Facebook Party style. See my chapter on <u>Online Opportunity Events</u> for more information, or the Facebook Parties section of *Social Media for Direct Selling Representatives.*

- Sometimes you do need to post an image that is promotional in nature, such as a new flier image for your seasonal product launch, the corporate image explaining a new starter kit special etc. Since Facebook negatively sanctions business sales posts in groups when they are administered by personal profiles, this can be problematic and land you in Facebook Jail. When you do need to post promotional images, I recommend posting them on a Business Page first—either your main public Business Page, or one you create just for this purpose, and then sharing from that post into your team group. This helps avoid any issues that may cause you to be perceived as "selling" within your group— even though those of us in the industry understand what you are doing is sharing a resource, the Facebook algorithm does not.

Facebook Groups for Prospecting and Marketing

This chapter has been focused on using Facebook Groups for supporting and training your team. However, this is a good place to mention the power of using Facebook Groups in marketing your business to meet new people and build your team. I would not recommend you create a group to attract new people—that is what Business Pages are for, as I explained in the first book. Some representatives like to use Facebook Groups to offer customer service to existing customers or hosts, and I see no problem with that as long as it is truly for customer service or community building, not selling.

But participating in other Facebook Groups as a way to meet new people and network, and possibly find your next new team member, is smart! There are many Facebook Groups based on various interests, among local people in your community, or focused on the direct selling business. Posting in these groups in a way that adds value or engages people in conversation without promoting your business is a great way to earn trust and rapport among those who may be looking for a new business. Establishing your expertise as a leader will attract prospects to you as well. Some groups are created specifically for sharing direct selling opportunities. Follow the guidelines of any group that you join and you might just find someone out there who is looking just for what you offer.

For More Information About Facebook Groups

General Facebook Groups Information:
groups.facebook.com

Help Center Group Questions:
facebook.com/help/www/162866443847527

Browse Other Facebook Groups to Join:
facebook.com/browsegroups

Online Team Meetings and Rallies

Having built my former career in the field primarily through people I met online, I know what it is like as a leader to rely on technology to build a sense of community among your team. If you don't find a way to gather people together online, your downline will end up feeling lonely and isolated, even if you are in touch with them individually on a regular basis. People want to belong to something bigger than themselves. They want to be part of the excitement, recognition and support that is so unique in the direct selling profession.

Why Hold Meetings Online Instead of—or in Addition to—In-Person Meetings?

- Online meetings give your long distance team a chance to connect with you and the others so you can truly be a team!

- They allow for structured training in a controlled environment that is recorded in some way to refer back to or reuse.

- People are often more open and outgoing online than in person. They are more comfortable sharing their ideas and celebrating their challenges or successes. This is especially true for the introverts on your team.

- It is convenient for both you, as a busy leader, and for your team. No need for a sitter, leaving the house, or dressing up.

- Online meetings are a fun way to build community among all your team members, near and far, not just the local ones or those who are able to travel to company events.

What Types of Meetings Can Be Held Virtually?

- Monthly or weekly general team meetings

- One-on-one or small group coaching/training on specific topics or for those working on promotions into leadership

- Half- or full-day (or even weekend!) virtual rallies

Also see my chapter on conducting Online Opportunity Events. Invite your team members to invite their own prospects to a team-wide income opportunity event.

Potential Challenges When Holding Online Team Meetings

Holding online meetings is not without its pitfalls. Below are a few you might run into.

- **Getting people to show up.** I recommend whichever platform you use, remind them often. I like using a Facebook event regardless of where the meeting is conducted online. This way if they RSVP Going or Interested/Maybe, they will get a reminder automatically.

- **Chatter/interruptions.** This happens at in-person meetings too. Sometimes it's a good idea to allow side conversations but when it is time to focus on training, or if there is a guest speaker, you will want to discourage that.

- **Technical difficulties.** I recommend that you practice using the platform you select, whether it is a Facebook Group or event, or live video streaming or something else. You can even create a secret Facebook Group or other platform account just for testing things.

- **Lack of face-to-face can feel impersonal.** Whenever possible, incorporate photographs of you or your team, or use recorded or live video. This really impacts the sense of community and personalizes your meeting.

- **Going overtime, being disorganized, or having a lack of structure.** Too often people say "it's meeting time" but aren't prepared with an agenda or a timeline. Always prepare an outline and keep track of time. Remember you are modeling good leadership for your team and that starts with managing your time well.

- **Your content is boring, so your team multitasks or doesn't really pay attention.** Keep it interesting and build in some interaction. Doing meetings online can feel passive, so it is easy for your team to just open the page and then keep doing other things because there is a computer or iPad between you. Keep them involved by asking questions or playing a game or inviting people to share.

Platforms for Online Team Meetings

Where you hold your meetings is up to you. Many people already have a Facebook Group for team support as mentioned in the prior chapter and will create an Event within the group set to a certain day or time and then conduct the meeting on the event page itself through posts or Facebook Live video. Some prefer to have a separate Facebook Group altogether where the separate group is only used for meetings. Then they invite everyone to the group and on a certain date or time they either go live on video or post a series of training posts in the group news feed or in albums.

Other social media sites where meetings can be conducted include a secret Pinterest board, or a private Instagram account. You can also conduct a meeting via Facebook's Messenger or some other messaging app that allows group conversations. If you are familiar with the Social Media Parties section in my first book, *Social Media for Direct Selling Representatives,* you know that social media can be great for sales events. When it comes to conducting online team meetings, you will want to make sure the platform you use allows the meeting to be closed or private. That said, I know many representatives who invite prospective team members to their online team meetings for a "sneak peek" into the support and training you offer before they've actually joined. I think this is a great idea, as long as you brief them in advance and follow up with them afterwards.

Another option is to use an outside tool such as a webinar or video meeting platform such as Zoom.us, AnyMeeting.com or Meet.fm. In these cases I would recommend inviting your team via a Facebook Event where you provide the link where they can join at the appropriate time, or invite and remind them by email.

Online Meeting Outline

I thought I would share my personal outline for online team meetings that I used when I was a field leader. You truly can build a loyal community and generate excitement about your company among your team through virtual meetings, and they are a great solution for teams spread out across the miles. I held online meetings every week, and they became a great way for everyone to gather and get energized about their businesses. If you are not up to doing them weekly, I would suggest at least monthly. I would also plan to delegate some of the duties or training, which allows you to develop more leaders under you as they gain experience through you.

Ideally the meeting will last about an hour, but the following agenda can be abbreviated for shorter gatherings. Include specific instructions for accessing the meeting when you send your invitations or set up your event, including whether phone or computer audio is required or if any special equipment or software is necessary if you are using one of the webinar style platforms.

The general theme of your meeting can be a simple open Q/A or Ask Me Anything, or coaching one or more consultants through challenges they are having, or featuring a guest expert, or offering training, recognition, and announcements from you or other team members.

This is the format I usually used:

1. Have someone record **attendance** if that isn't built into your system.

2. **On-Time Drawing.** Thank everyone for coming and being on time. Have someone else (or use something like random.org) pick a number to choose someone to win the "On-Time Drawing" and offer a small prize such as a supply item that you mail to the winner. If you are doing weekly meetings this can add up so I would recommend modeling for your team to keep this simple/inexpensive.

3. **Introduction/Announcements**. If there are new people, briefly introduce yourself as the leader, then remind everyone of company promotions/incentives that are going on,

or anything they need to be aware of (and may not have read in the company emails or back office!)

4. **Success Story**. Schedule this person ahead of time, or if no one is scheduled, explain it and ask for volunteers. This can be someone sharing something they tried that worked, or sharing their Why Story, or something inspirational. Ask the guest to be specific so others can relate, or even duplicate what they've done.

5. **Recognition for the week or month**. You can use standard numbers that you get in your reports, but in my experience, the more personalized you can make it, the more effective it will be. Recognize something they aren't necessarily going to read in the company news. Perhaps you can tie this into the previous meeting's training. For example, if the last training was on booking shows, recognize who has booked the most new shows since the last meeting. Try recognizing someone who has reached a personal goal, or those who achieved a company incentive. Whatever you do recognize, encourage everyone to cheer for each person in some way. "Let's all give Susie a round of applause!" Even though you are on the computer or mobile devices, your team will get creative in giving Susie the shout-outs she deserves! They will post emoji or stickers, or simply say "Way to go!" This is fun for everyone.

6. **Training Topic**. For your training, it can be typing, or posting a picture with a caption explaining it, or it could be you demonstrating or explaining something on live video, showing something on a PDF or presentation (try linking to something in your Google drive), playing a pre-recorded video, or using a screen sharing tool. Throughout the train-

ing whenever you can, ask a simple question to keep it interactive, either for them to share ideas, or a pop quiz type question.

7. **Trivia game.** This is just one game idea for a fun meeting. Ask them questions about the company, the comp plan, the hostess program etc. Give them "points" for answering first correctly (you will have to record these with tally marks on paper the old fashioned way,) and the one with the most points wins a prize. Try delegating the points tally to someone on your team.

8. **Question/Answer Time.** Let them pick your brain or get ideas from others. You can restrict it to this meeting's topic or leave it open, depending on how much time is left.

9. **End with a WOW.** Have your team share what is one thing they will commit to accomplishing Within One Week. Have them type it in right there for all to see.

10. **Remind** them of the next meeting and say goodbye!

11. Be sure to **mail the prize** to your drawing winner!

Conduct a Half or Full Day "Virtual Rally"

Want to hold a longer meeting or mini-conference with your own line? Virtual Rallies are fun and fast paced half or full days of training online! Use your regular online meeting tool and be sure to invite everyone well in advance. Explain that you will be spending the day (or half the day) on the computer together.

Be sure to gather RSVPs in some way so you can send out reminders and instructions. A Facebook Event works well for this but you can even send postcards, emails or use a tool like the app Redstamp to make it extra special.

I conducted these once or twice a year, typically around the time of convention or just after, or during new product launches.

Invite leaders or strong consultants who have an area of expertise to be guest trainers on topics such as host coaching, sponsoring, party game ideas, phone calling, and so on. Offer a gift (such as a supply item or product) to your guest trainers as a thank-you. If you have a newer team, consider inviting someone from another line to help you out or even someone from outside your company in exchange for a couple of minutes at the end to share their product/service.

Be sure to publicize your event in your newsletters, blog, Facebook Group, etc. You can't remind people too much – you will really want to have good attendance so they all receive the training. Keep it top of mind so they are excited to come and don't want to be left out!

Encourage your guest trainers to create handouts, then post those online either in your Facebook Group Files area, or in Google Drive or Dropbox, and email the sharing link to everyone either before or after the event. On my team, we would create a separate web page on my team blog site for each Virtual Rally and they could find all the information about topics and agenda as well as handouts and links to the recordings there. If you are using a Facebook Group I recommend setting everything up in a new document in the Files area and/or using an Album so it is easy to find later.

Have training sessions on the hour, for twenty or fifty minutes with a five or ten minute break between topics. Start with a fifteen minute introductory session where you explain the agenda for the day, how to participate, etc. Encourage everyone to get up and stretch during the breaks so they can be more attentive during the trainings.

At the end of each session, or every so often, you could give away an inexpensive door prize by playing a short game or picking a random number. For example if the number is 7 you would look at your attendee list and #7 in line is the winner. Announce the winner and mail them their gift.

End the Virtual Rally with a "Virtual Banquet" where people can share their "aha's" for the day, or you can offer up more recognition or special announcements. We took a break just before the "banquet" and I would playfully tell them to change into their evening gowns! You could even have them actually do this and post a picture. How fun!

We also took a "team portrait" at the end for fun—this was just a screen shot of everyone typing "goodbye" into the chat! It was a silly and fun way to end the day and something to mark the special event. I would then post this picture on our team website or social media.

Online Team Meeting Topic Ideas

As you are aware, there are many leaders in your company that they could choose to join under—but they chose you! Sometimes this is intentional, sometimes it is circumstantial and sometimes it is a complete accident! However, as their leader, it is your duty to provide guidance and model behaviors that lead to success.

Answering the following questions can help you wrap your head around some ideas for content, social media posts or training that you can provide for your team, aligning with your own leadership values as well as their needs. Following the questions are some training topic ideas that may be helpful as well.

1. What is your leadership persona or avatar? If someone were to ask others on your team what you are like as a leader, what would they say?

2. What are your five core personal values that you wish to uphold and exemplify in your leadership?

3. What are five to ten challenges that your ideal new or veteran team member face for which you might be able to provide guidance?

4. Which of your team's challenges are areas that you or your company can guide them to resolve through personal coaching or training?

5. What are five to ten resources you have at your disposal you can share with your team members?

There are a variety of ways I've offered for how to actually deliver your coaching and training, whether it is through a live training online or by posting images with training topics, or creating pre-recorded videos. Now, here are some ideas for topics you may want to address. Whenever possible, I recommend reinforcing your company's existing training that they may be providing. That way your team learns that there are many resources already available to them. It does not make sense for you, as a busy leader, to reinvent the wheel when it is not necessary!

However, where your company training may be lacking, consider developing or referring your team to training on these topics. I enjoyed the creativity involved in offering weekly training to my team and I felt that it helped keep things fresh in my personal business, too! So if any of these aren't areas where you feel confident, perhaps it would be a fun project for you to learn more about it and implement it yourself as you develop your training.

- Writing/saying your "why" story

- Discovering your business values

- Practicing your introduction/thirty-second commercial for networking

- How to share success stories/testimonials

- How to handle questions/pushback

- How to write compelling private messages

- Goal setting/business planning

- Following up with guests/prospects

- How to network in online and offline groups

- Increasing attendance/reducing cancelations at offline and online parties

- How to demonstrate a product

- The art of up-selling or selling in bundles

- Managing your time/life balance

- Company mission/history education

- Creating a productive in-home office space

- Getting more party bookings from your parties

- Getting party bookings outside of parties

- Vendor booth training (lead collection/follow up/displays)

- Involving your family/getting support from your spouse

- How to have conversations that lead to business

- Developing or maximizing fundraisers
- How to keep business going in _____ month/season
- Host coaching for online or offline parties
- Customer loyalty/customer service
- Creative sales or booking ideas
- Common mistakes in direct sales
- Courage/motivation
- How to get out of a slump
- Stretching your comfort zone
- Professionalism/image and appearance in business
- Compliance training/P&P training
- Asking for and getting referrals
- Consistency/calendaring
- Inbox management/email management
- Getting organized (paperwork/taxes)
- How-to training: back office, website, putting in orders, etc.
- Sponsoring everywhere/always be listening
- Party game ideas for online and offline sales parties
- Latest trends around your topic/product line
- How to use technology (social media, apps, online tools)
- On-boarding new consultants

Developing Leadership Skills

In addition to this book and my prior book, *Social Media for Direct Selling Representatives*, there are some independent direct selling trainers and coaches I respect and who I know provide excellent training that you may want to access when needed to build up your own foundation, especially for non-technology-related knowledge. Some of them offer the opportunity to hire them as guest trainers for your team on their topics like I do.

Trainers I admire as colleagues today or who influenced my own direct selling leadership experience are Michelle Archer from The Direct Sales Institute, Deb Bixler from the Cash Flow Show Direct Sales Radio, Belinda Ellsworth from Step Into Success, Beth Jones-Schall from Spirit of Success, Becky Spieth from Leaders Empowered and Mary Christensen, author of many direct selling books including *Be a Network Marketing Leader*, to which I am a contributor. Although I only chose to list a few among many excellent colleagues out there, know that in addition to the support and guidance your own company and upline leaders may provide, it is often beneficial to look outside for excellent supplemental advice on running your business as a leader.

Blogging for Leaders

A blog is a website where you have the opportunity to add articles, called "posts," that appear on the site usually in the order of most recently written to oldest. The blog itself is dynamic. You write a new post, it appears at the top, and pushes the other posts down, similarly to how the news feeds work on social media sites. Usually readers find your articles or see them shared in social media and they comment, usually on the bottom of the post itself. Sometimes articles can lead to lively discussions among readers and a sense of community can be formed. In addition to the blog posts, you can usually also create "static" pages that remain fixed in place, such as the home page, or in the menu bar or navigation. These are called "pages" instead of "posts" and usually include things such as the About page and informational pages. Blogs usually have "widgets," which are functions you can insert in the side bar or top or bottom of the general layout such as a search box or an archive of posts, or a logo or picture of the author.

For leaders, it is common to create a general blog website that has some information about the leader and the opportunity on the home page, or on the About page. Then you can have another page that is something of a "team login" that is password-protected. The leader can then give her team the web address and password to this private area and once logged in, they can access additional pages such as shared files, training articles, or videos.

Creating Your Team Blog

Should you start a website or blog so that you can use it to attract business and support your team? *The first thing to look into is whether your company allows it.* Many companies do not allow representatives to create stand-alone websites that might compete or conflict with the company-provided replicated website or that may put them at risk when representatives do not follow compliance guidelines. You may have restrictions about whether you can link to your company website or mention your company name at all. You may also be limited in how you are able to market or promote this self-created website.

It is very important, especially as a leader, that you follow your company Policies and Procedures regarding Internet marketing and websites, blogs, and social media. Following your P&P to the letter helps maintain the integrity of the very opportunity you are offering to others.

Companies have valid reasons for placing restrictions on representatives, many times due to potential legal complications or past experience with "rogue distributors" doing things that were problematic. Sometimes they simply prefer to have more control over the branding and messaging and sometimes they just prefer the company site to be the website "hub" that leads customers to the right person. Regardless of the reason, always respect your company's stand on these things, and if you are curious or want to understand more, contact your compliance department and start a conversation instead of simply finding a way around it.

No one really "needs" to blog, in the same way that no one really "needs" to be on social media. Plenty of leaders, and teams large and small, thrive without ever creating a team website or blog or even one for their own personal business. Since I have seen many companies who have rules against separate websites, I hesitated to include this information in this book as I do not want anyone to think that creating a stand-alone website is necessary for success — it really is not.

However, if your company does allow its representatives or leaders to create a blog or a support site such as a team blog, and you have the inclination to do so, I decided it would be better to include that information than to exclude it.

For the purposes of this book, I am talking about a website or blog (or more accurately, a website that is based on a blogging platform) created specifically for the purpose of you expressing yourself as a leader, and for the support of your team. Perhaps you can include some introductory information about your income opportunity, in case others find the website and want to learn more.

Starting a blog or team site may be a bit daunting, as it does require some time and skills to get going and may feel like "one more thing" for you to learn, do and maintain. This task can be one where you may choose to hire someone to get it started, and maybe even maintain it for you while you provide the content. As a busy leader this makes a lot of sense, but if you prefer to do it yourself, I have provided instructions below.

Again, having a blog is not necessary, and every business is different. But if you are curious, here are some reasons you may want to consider creating one.

Benefits of Blogging

- Blog articles are indexed by the search engines as if they were each their own independent website. This means that if you post even just 1 new article a week, you are creating 52 new and completely independent doorways into your business, year after year. If you are writing articles that people are searching for, you will get new traffic and new business, and the articles stay on the web indefinitely. Over time, you will create a tremendous bank of material and ways people can find you.

- More than likely your company provides you with a replicated website for selling products and advertising your services, such as in home or virtual parties or your income opportunity. That website does not usually afford you much space to express yourself, or for potential customers to get to know you as an individual separate from the company branding. Blogging is one way to share your thoughts, feelings, opinions, ideas and education with your prospects and customers. When they get to know you, they will like you, trust you, and more readily do business with you.

- You have an unlimited amount of space in which to write in a blog. Social media posts are great, especially with today's "short attention spans." However, when you really need to explain something or expand on a thought, a blog is a great place to do that. You can always post a short teaser in social media, with a link to your blog for those who want to read more.

- When you use a self-hosted blogging platform (meaning that you subscribe to an outside website hosting service on which the blog exists) such as the self-hosted version of WordPress.org, you are in total control. In social media, there are rules and if you read the Terms of Service carefully, when you post on social media sites, you are giving the site permission to use your content any way they like. In your own self-hosted blog, you are the sole owner of your intellectual property. I should note here that there are some non-self-hosted options as well (simply referred to as hosted blogging platforms) where you may not have the same ownership advantage. However, they do give you a relatively easy and cost-free way to blog, but without the custom domain you would have with an outside website hosting service.

- You are also in control of how your blog looks and feels, including having the layout or graphics match your personal or company branding. No one is going to change the layout except you, so there are no surprises.

- Blogs are flexible and adaptable. With self-hosted WordPress blogs you can add seemingly limitless functionality through plugins and widgets, depending on your company's goals and specific needs. Want to display a calendar, or share files? Want a video that stays on the top in the sidebar? How about an email newsletter opt-in box or freebie giveaway as a lead generator front and center? All of these can be accomplished with a few clicks and can be rearranged any way you like, anytime.

- Creating at least one blog post a week gives you content that you and your readers can share across other social networks. Add "social sharing" buttons on each article, and not only can you easily share to your own social media sites, but readers through the years will share to their networks as well.

- Blog articles establish expertise and authority on your topic. In business today, it is important to serve up information around topics that your ideal customer or client would be interested in, so that you become the go-to resource or authority on that topic. Because of this, people will think of you when they need your product or service. When you write articles, opinion pieces, how-to's and inspiring stories around your topic, others will read, share and comment on your articles, resulting in your credibility on the topic you choose or within the direct selling industry goes up.

- Leaders who use blog articles to answer frequently asked questions — or provide solutions for common problems — demonstrate great customer service! We all seem to have those questions that many people ask us again and again. Writing articles addressing those questions not only serves those who are asking the questions, but it also serves those you haven't met yet but who are seeking answers in the search engines if your posts are public. It even makes it easier for your team members to start training their own teams.

Blogging can be a creative outlet! Although it may seem daunting at first — getting all the technical parts in order — once that is done, you may find you actually enjoy writing each week! Many leaders have been pleasantly surprised to find how good it feels to write, even though they never would have considered themselves a writer! Creativity feeds success, and writing can be one way to get creative in your business.

What Platform Options Are There?

- **WordPress.org**. I mentioned self-hosted WordPress.org blogs earlier and that has always been my preference. In fact I started my training business teaching people how to use WordPress! It will always be my first love when it comes to social media. There is a cost to secure hosting (about $100 a year or less) but it is worth it to have the control over your visibility on "owned" territory vs. "rented" space. That said, there are some other options that some people like to use, and they might even be a good place to start while you get used to the idea and start writing, getting your message out there in a bigger way than traditional social media provides. You may even want to start a blog on a non-business topic at first, such as a recipe-sharing site, a travelogue or some other more personal topic. Then, when you are ready to blog on a professional level, open up your self-hosted site. For team blogs, I still prefer WordPress.org. It is a good idea, no matter which platform you choose, to make sure you have the option to make some posts or pages private when needed. I like the idea of giving your team access to your site with one password that will work on any of the private posts. If you only want to create a team support blog, but do not want to do a public-facing site for visibility or sponsoring, you can even make your entire site password protected.

- **WordPress.com** The dot-com version of WordPress is a hosted blogging platform where your blog "lives" on the server along with thousands of others. Although you can get your own URL or domain name, it is simply a "mask" for the sub-domain of WordPress.com, and there will be a fee from WordPress.com for that privilege. At one point,

WordPress.com came out against direct selling as "work from home schemes," so I would caution you against using this platform for any outward selling or sponsoring. Instead, think of it more as an information-sharing site, team support or personal blog. The advantage of using Word-Press.com is that it easily converts to WordPress.org, the self-hosted version, when you are ready to make it more professional and business-friendly. WordPress.org has no restrictions on selling or sponsoring since you own the site that is housed on a third party hosting service.

- **Blogger.com** also known as Blogspot. This is one of the original blogging platforms and has a strong social component in that other Blogger users will follow and comment on each other's posts. Like WordPress.com, this is a hosted service, not self-hosted, so the site you create will operate as a sub-domain. Sub-domains or hosted blogs tend to not perform as well in the search engines since the main domain or URL has the most authority. Blogger is now owned by Google so that *should* give you an advantage like YouTube does, but I have not seen that to be true. Again, it is not designed for business use, so it is better to use as an informational or personal blog.

- **Medium.com** This is one of the newest blogging platforms that has been gaining ground recently because news outlets, public figures—and what we call "influencers" or "thought leaders"—have been using it. It seems to perform well in the search engines, even better than the prior two options above, but not as well as self-hosted WordPress sites. Medium's best two features are that your readers can insert comments alongside the pertinent part of your post instead of only commenting below it, and that Medium itself is more like a social network where you can subscribe to authors you like, which creates a feed of recently posted articles where friends can comment and share easily. For this reason, it is very easy to attract new followers and increase your visibility. Medium is a great choice for those who tend toward opinion pieces, storytelling, or topics that appeal to the general population vs. a very specific and narrow focus.

- There are other blog-style platforms that many leaders are successfully using but I do not personally use. Since they are less popular for business purposes and are not as search-engine-friendly as the options I mentioned above, they may be fine for a beginner or for someone who really is not concerned with their team blog being found online or having some of the features the others provide. Such sites are those provided by Weebly, Wix, TypePad and Tumblr.

How Do I Get Started Creating a Self-Hosted WordPress Blog?

If I were to attempt to teach you all the features and capabilities of WordPress.org blogs it would mean writing another entire book. For the purposes of this edition, which is geared toward direct selling leaders who might want to create a blog for sponsoring or supporting their team, I will keep it brief. I do have a short video course called Blogging for Beginners—ask me about it if you are interested in that!

This is a good time to clarify that the type of blog I am discussing here is a stand-alone blog or site. Since most direct sellers will have a website provided by their company that they cannot edit or append a blog, a stand-alone blog is probably the only option. If you are reading this and have a regular small business with your own website already, but do not have a blog, you would simply create a page on your website called "Blog" and link it to your blog, which is set up separately. It is always best if your blog is hosted in the same place as your website but since this is not an option for replicated direct sales websites, we are focusing on stand-alone blogs.

If you choose to use WordPress.org, my preferred type of blog, here is how you would go about it:

1. Secure WordPress-friendly blog hosting. If you are not sure, ask customer service if they cater to WordPress users since some of them do not and things may be difficult. I prefer HostGator, DreamHost, Bluehost or the "king" of paid WordPress hosting, WPEngine.

2. Purchase a domain name either from your hosting company or an outside domain registrar. I use NameCheap.com but there are many other reputable companies where you can purchase your domain name.

3. Follow your host's directions for how to direct your domain name to your hosting company. This usually involves your host providing you with some code that needs to be copy/pasted into settings on your domain account. This ensures that when someone types your domain name URL into their browser, it pulls up your site.

4. To install WordPress you can either go to the WordPress.org site and follow the manual installation instructions to download the software and install it into your hosting account, or you can use an automatic service that is usually provided within your hosting account. Most I've seen are called Quick-Install though your host may have a different name for it. This is usually the easiest. Once you have it set up, the WordPress dashboard on your site may instruct you to up-

date to the most current version, which only takes a few clicks. When you are installing WordPress, make sure you read all the instructions and every email they send you and follow directions. By the way, you will be asked to give your blog a title and possibly a subtitle. Be sure to delete the default subtitle that says "Just another WordPress blog."

5. Once your site is installed and "live" you will see that WordPress gave you a basic layout or "theme" to work with. These can easily be changed in your dashboard. Visit the Appearance tab and look at the themes (layouts) available and click Add New to explore further and install a new one. You can change your theme any time while you are experimenting and before you publicize your site. There are outside sources where you can find WordPress themes, but I recommend only using those that are either sanctioned by WordPress (in their theme directory) or paid versions such as Headway, Genesis or Divi by Elegant Themes.

6. Go to Settings and then Permalinks in your dashboard. Choose the Custom option and type in this format: /%postname%/. This will make sure that each post's web address will highlight the words in the post title without all the extras like category or post date, which dilute the keywords and complicate the URL.

7. Go to the Pages tab in your dashboard. Click on Add New and create a Welcome or home page of some sort. You will see an editing bar with options for inserting pictures or formatting your text and other options. This page will serve as your homepage, so include any kind of message you would like people to see when they first land on your blog. Be sure to *save* it!

8. Go back to the Pages tab and find the sample About page. Click on Edit and change it to your own About information, such as a bio and maybe a picture and save.

9. Go to the Pages tab again and click Add New and create a page with the title of Blog — and nothing else and then save it.

10. Go to your Settings tab and then the Reading sub-tab, and change the settings to show the Front Page as the welcome page you created, and the Posts Page to show the blog page you created. This will make it so your introductory message opens as the home page with a tab on the top or side to access your blog. Some people prefer to have their blog posts show up as their front page, but I find this confusing as far as branding. If they do not yet know you, it will be more difficult to find out who you are and what you do, since the first thing they see would be your most recent post, which may or may not make those things clear. Always be sure to save your work!

11. Next go to the Posts tab in your dashboard. This is where your blog posts or articles will live. There will already be a sample post called "Hello World" in the list of posts. Click Move to Trash to delete this.

12. Go to the Comments tab on your dashboard and find the sample comment that WordPress installed and delete it, too!

13. Go to the Appearance tab in your dashboard and find the Widgets tab. Widgets are sections that appear either in your sidebar or in the footer of your site which adds functionality to your blog. This is how you can add things such as images or search boxes, a list of topic categories or your lat-

est blog post titles. Click to drag and drop the widgets you would like to have on your site, then adjust any settings for that widget and save. If you would like something that doesn't appear in the options you can try adding what they call a plugin to download a new widget. Do that by finding the Plugins tab and then click on Add New and search on what you want — including the word "widget" — then view the details and follow instructions to add it to your site if you like it.

14. Now go to your Plugins tab in your dashboard and activate the Akismet plugin. Plugins are additional functionality for your site. Usually they are things that operate in the background, though some of them do affect the appearance of your site, such as some widgets. See below for a list of plugins I like. Akismet is a spam prevention tool that will help weed out any spam comments. You will need to follow all instructions and Akismet will ask you for a donation — though it is free for personal blog use — so you can select 0 if you wish. If you plan to do any sales on your site it is a professional courtesy to donate to them, since they are providing a much-needed service!

15. Now you're ready to create your first blog post! Click on the Posts tab and then Add New.

16. Give your post a nice title with words that people might search for, and then start writing your post. I recommend it be at least 350 words, but 500 or more is best so that the search engines see it as quality content.

17. You can insert pictures whenever appropriate — use the little photograph icon to do this. Images will be stored in your Media tab in your dashboard. It is best to include the title

and descriptive words in the alternate text for each image so that if someone who is visually impaired loads your site, they will be able to have their text-reading software tell them what the image is about. These additional words also help the search engines know what your post is about since they do not read images, only text.

18. When your post content feels ready, look to the right side and find the area that says Category. Consider what types of post topics you might be writing about in your blog and plan on using different categories for them. You will be assigning each post to a certain category, which allows your readers to find your posts by the topics they may be interested in. For example, one category might be "Working from Home." Another might be "All About ABC Company." Another might be "Support for My Team." You can include other topics related to your business or favorite topics such as recipes, fashion trends, workout ideas etc. Think of categories as the file drawer your articles might go into — they are broad topics. When you first write a post and do not have Categories set up, you simply choose Add New in the Categories section and type one in to assign it.

19. Next find the Tags section under Categories on the right. Tags are like sub-topics, maybe the file folders in that file drawer where the posts themselves would be the papers filed into a particular folder. They are more specific topics and again, will be used over and over. For example, if you have a Recipes category, your tags might be chicken, dinner, casserole. I recommend three to five tags. These may or may not show up visibly on your post under the title, depending on your theme's settings. They do, however, alert

the search engines as to what your post is about, in the same way the Category and Title will.

Now you are ready to either click the Publish button, save the post as a draft that you can edit later, or next to the publishing date on the top right, click on Edit to edit the publishing date and schedule your post to go "live" at a specific time in the future. This makes it easy to queue up posts to always go out on certain days. Ta dah! You're a blogger!

Plugins I Like

There are a variety of plugins you can add to your blog to increase functionality or effectiveness. In the plugins tab click on Add New and type words into the search bar to find things you may want to add. It is a good idea to not only look at the details of each one, but to also check the reviews. Plugins with poor reviews are best avoided, of course. In addition, sometimes plugins are not compatible with your theme or other plugins, so be sure to read all of the details. Following are some of the basic plugins I currently use and there are many others to choose from — as well as more advanced plugins when you are ready. I just happen to like these and think they are useful:

- **Custom Share Buttons with Floating Sidebar by MR Web Solution.** Adds buttons to posts or pages that allow your readers to share to their social networks.

- **TinyMCE Advanced by Andrew Ozz.** Adds more editing buttons to the publishing editor.

- **Revive Old Post by Codeinwp.** Recycles your public blog posts by posting them to Twitter regularly.

- **Contact Form 7 by Takayuki Miyoshi.** Allows you to customize contact forms where people can request more information about your business or income opportunity.

- **Yoast SEO by Yoast/Joost de Valk.** Makes it easy to increase search engine visibility to posts.

- **Smush Image Compression by WPMU DEV.** Makes your large images load faster.

- **The Events Calendar by Modern Tribe.** List all your upcoming events/trainings.

Additional Tips for Marketing Your Blog

If it has been established that you are allowed to have a blog where you cannot only support your team but also market your business, it is important to know that you cannot simply build the blog and expect people to find you. The search engines look for at least three things when evaluating websites to list. Blogs cater to all three:

- Quantity of unique and relevant content

- The newness or freshness of the content

- The link structure surrounding the website (links to your site, and links from your site to others)

The following tasks will help your blog get found — if that is what you wish!

1. Remember my Social Media CPR method? The same formula works for blogging as well. **Comment** on three to five other blogs, **Post** something new on your blog on a regular basis that is mostly helpful, useful and interesting content with a little bit of selling and sponsoring occasionally — and maybe even something personal or casual too. **Reply** to

comments either on your own posts or in response to comments you made on others' blogs. It works.

2. Write blog posts that would be interesting to those in your target market. For direct selling leaders who are hoping to either attract or support new team members, think about topics that would be useful to new direct sellers. What might they need to learn?

3. Link out to other resources within your posts. This gives your blog authority and also adds a social element. Email the other blog you may be linking to, letting them know. Who knows? They may be so honored that they share your post!

4. Link TO your blog on your social media profiles, in your newsletter, and when commenting on others' blog posts. If you follow other (non-competitor) blogs, it is always valuable to comment on posts you read. When you do, you are usually given the option to list your name and website which will then be clickable in your comment.

5. List your blog in popular blog directories:

   - blogs.botw.org

   - dmoz.org

   - BlogCatalog.com

6. Subscribe to or follow the top blogs in your field. Learn from them. Use them as a springboard for ideas to blog about yourself. Get clear about what you enjoy and like about them.

7. Set up Google Alerts to keep track of hot topics your readers might enjoy. You can either link to those items, adding

some additional opinions and thoughts within a post, or you might be inspired to write completely new articles on some of those same topics. Google Alerts is a system that will email you a daily digest of articles or blog posts about any topic you choose. Set this up at google.com/alerts.

8. Blog about hot topics in direct sales or your particular company's topic, linking to others blogging about that topic. For example, if you see that the latest thing in direct selling is a new strategy you already know about, blog about it! Think of this as doing a "current events" report. Talking about something that is on everyone's mind is a valuable way to be discovered while people are searching for that topic.

9. Search social bookmarking sites on your tags/keywords and see which blog posts are bookmarked most frequently. Add your own posts to the social bookmarking sites. One I like is StumbleUpon.

10. Actively participate in conversations on other blogs. Always check the box that allows you to be notified of additional comments so that you can jump back into the conversation any time.

11. And of course, as I mentioned before, comment and reply on your own blog posts and comments. Beware of the "spam" comments you may get in your pending comments folder in your dashboard. However, whenever you have an authentic and relevant comment to approve, always go to that post and reply back to the person. They will appreciate the response and feel "seen" while also being more likely to return.

Blog Post Topics that Establish You as a Leader and Direct Selling Resource

Some general topics you can customize to your situation or business are listed below. Important note: do not twist these into an "ad" post! Share authentically about your own life, or people you know, making sure that you reflect these themes or aspects of having a home-based business with your company. Each of these broader topics could have many other small parts that can become individual posts. The idea here is to serve those reading your posts with mostly informative topics, and a few promotional blog posts mixed in (sound familiar?)

Non-Promotional:

- The freedom and flexibility you enjoy

- Friends you meet in the business and as customers

- Incentives you have earned

- Personal growth from being in direct sales

- Accomplishing challenges/achieving goals

- Paying for your child's (education, dance class, summer camp etc.)

- Paying for (home remodel, new car, refrigerator) with your business money

- How to achieve "life balance" working from home

- How to choose a direct sales company

- Share your "why" or "I" story

- Steps to starting a business

- What to do to prepare for success in your business

- How to work from home with kids underfoot

- What is direct sales/how does it work

- What are the tax benefits to working from home

- How to choose a sponsor to join under

- How to be effective in direct sales in general

- Share articles/posts/photos/videos others create

Promotional:

- What is included in your kit—link to info

- Any specials or incentives you or the company are running about the business opportunity

- What makes you different/unique as a leader—why they should join your team

- Specific info about your company's career plan, requirements, etc.

- Company history or mission

- Anything specifically related to your company or linked to your website

When I first started teaching Internet marketing, I was conducting hands-on blogging classes in my local area. I have lots of experience working with entrepreneurs one-on-one to get their blogs started, and I've been there when they felt like tearing their hair out, too! I understand that this chapter may be a bit overwhelming for some. You are not alone.

That said, I thought it was important enough of a topic to include here and I would invite you to stretch yourself and try it. As the world becomes smaller every day with the increased reach of social media, it is important to have a place where you truly own the content, where no one can move it around or take it away but you, where no one benefits financially from your words but you. Whether using your blog for marketing your personal business or for supporting your team, I hope you will find it is a worthwhile endeavor!

Video for Marketing and Training

Back in 2012 I heard a social media influencer predict that within three years video would be the number one most important way to market your business. At that time, many people were skeptical about his assertion. After all, most of us were still used to consuming television on actual televisions, not on Netflix or Apple TV on our computers or other devices. YouTube was very popular already, but when it came to social media, most people were still scrolling through and reading status updates, and maybe clicking a link here and there. The thought of having to stop what we were doing to watch and listen to a video felt almost invasive.

Well, as you can imagine, the doubters were wrong and his prediction came true. Now, not only do people consume more and more video via social media or through computers, for many of us, it is nearly the only way we view video content! Social media sites have adjusted settings so we can watch with or without sound, auto-play or not, and they have even begun adding closed-captioning. Video is not the future — it's the present. All the popular social media sites are also rewarding video

with increased visibility in the feeds. which means for marketing, creating video is where it's at. With the advent of native
live streaming on Facebook, Instagram and Twitter, video is
helping us connect on a more personal and relatable level that
truly helps you build stronger relationships. It is as if you are
right there in someone's home having a conversation! I am excited to see where video takes us next as the social media world
continues to improve on this. For now, I recommend that you,
as leaders, learn how to use both pre-recorded video that you
then host on YouTube, and live video such as that available on
Facebook Live. This chapter will give you some basics for doing
these things.

General Tips for Leaders Using Video

- When doing any kind of presentation or training, it is always a good idea to practice. I know that when you see
  others doing video, they make it look so easy, but it can be
  pretty stressful without practice! I recommend you setting
  up a private Facebook Group for yourself where you (or
  you and a trusted friend) are the only members. This way
  you cannot only practice the technology, such as with Facebook Live, but you can see how things look from the
  viewer's standpoint and possibly get some feedback. If you
  are using YouTube, you can set your video to Secret before
  uploading it and then no one can see it but you or those you
  send it to. Sometimes there are certain things you might
  want to change that you would not have noticed until after
  uploading the final video—such as seeing that there is a lag
  in the audio, which appeared to be fine while you were recording it!

- Speaking of audio, for most computers and smart phones, as long as you are pretty close to the mic, the audio is okay to use as is. However, those mics don't usually block out background noise, which can be a distraction, — even if it is as subtle as a paper rattling as you look at your notes. For this reason, I usually recommend, at the very least, using your basic earbuds with a built-in mic. You really don't need to use something fancy like an external microphone if you don't want to, though they can really help too! If you like to be a little further away from the camera you can even get a mic extension cord. And since you do not need to actually be able to hear anything when you are recording or going live in most cases, you can simply get a lapel mic that plugs into your mic jack and those work well also.

- Lighting is another thing to consider. After audio, it can be one of the most critical components when making a video, whether it is pre-recorded or live, in your home office or out and about. One of the most important — and the easiest things to fix if your lighting isn't great — is to be sure the light is on your face, not behind you. Sometimes this means placing your computer or smartphone in a completely different part of the room, and sometimes it simply means turning the overhead light off and lighting up a desk lamp in front of you. If you are lucky, you can simply face an exterior window and achieve a nice healthy glow! In my home office the lighting is typically dark, so I use some lighting equipment to help me out such as a ring light on a stand, and a mini version on my phone.

- I always recommend having a basic bullet point outline nearby, not necessarily a script. Having an outline easily visible to you will help you make sure you do not leave something important out, such as what you want your viewers to do next, or asking if there are any questions. Decide on a format you would like, such as videos of your team meetings or opportunity events, an interview with someone else, general thoughts of the day, a class where you are teaching a new skill, a question/answer session, a coaching hot seat, general discussion, company news, broadcasting company or team events, sharing some inspiration, addressing a current issue going on, sharing a demonstration or product or business explanation. If you need the ability to have more than one person on the video, you can do that through recording a Zoom.us meeting or try going live with BeLive.tv, which allows you to stream two people on Facebook Live. If you do decide to include others, train them on the platform and do a test run first. These are great ways to have other team members or special guests offer additional training for your team.

- The length of videos has fluctuated over time and the general consensus these days is to keep training videos under fifteen minutes, and to keep marketing videos at under five, but closer to one or two minutes. This is difficult for those of us with a lot to say! But I've found it is better to keep it short and sweet and then come back with a second or third video on another topic, rather than overwhelm people who will not have time to sit and watch the traditional 30-60 minute show. Viewers of live broadcasts, such as through Facebook Live, tend to tolerate longer video as long as you are giving most of the valuable information at the beginning. Even if you are recording a live streaming video, most people watch the recording later and aren't going to appreciate having to scroll through a longer video, which brings me to another subject.

- Invite people to view your videos or your live stream in a variety of ways. You can simply post to your page or group to "save the date" and come back for the video or you can use a Facebook Event to do the inviting. And don't forget about "old fashioned" email or Evites! I really like the application Redstamp, which you can use to email or text beautifully designed invitations and reminders to people. This can work well for trainings. Private messaging, texting or emailing work just fine, too.

- When you start your video, look at the camera (not at yourself on the screen, since that isn't always where the camera is!) and then get to the point. Pretend like you are speaking to just one person and looking them in the eye. In my opinion, there is no need for you to do a long introduction or explain what you are going to explain, and then explain it and then review what you explained! Shorter videos are more powerful and long intros or fillers will frustrate some of your viewers. Provide value immediately. If it is live, do not wait around for viewers to show up. Get right to the content and after you have provided some value, then it is appropriate to introduce yourself briefly.

- I also do not personally care for the style of live video broadcast where the presenter interrupts her message by greeting each person as they come online. This is distracting to others and dilutes your authority. If you would like to have a social aspect to your video I recommend waiting till a break halfway through, or waiting till the end and opening it up for questions/comments. This way, those who are there for the training will be able to access the important information right away and can choose to turn it off later if they are short on time.

- Last, but not least, when your video is done or your broadcast is over, be sure to keep or download the source file so you can repurpose it in other places. If it was a Facebook Live video and appropriate to share, upload it to your YouTube channel and if you have a team blog, embed it into a blog post. Then share to your other social networks for extra coverage. If, on your live broadcast, you dove into specific topics that need more explaining, edit the caption to include more information, or add images and short videos into the comments of the main video. Make it easy for people to get the most value out of each time you post a video. They will appreciate it!

Equipment Needed to Create Videos

- Smartphone, tablet or laptop (depending on which platform you are using)

- Webcam (built in, smartphone or tablet, or external such as Logitech)

- A tripod and an adapter to attach your smartphone is a good idea — if you are using your phone! I use a lightweight Acuvar tripod and the iOgrapher rig to attach my phone in landscape mode.

- Microphone (earbuds with mic, built-in mic (in your smartphone, tablet or laptop; or external such as Blue Yeti, AudioTechnica, or Snowball)

- Lighting (in front of you, such as Diva Ring, Chatlight, Neewer or another selfie light)

- Backdrop or suitable decor that will show up behind you. If need be, hang a sheet or shower curtain up. People's eyes will wander, so your background is important.

- Excellent Internet connection (hardwired is best for computer-based video, or make sure you have a good wi-fi or data signal for mobile apps.)

Here are some specifics about using pre-recorded video on YouTube, or going Live on Facebook:

Your YouTube Channel

Did you know that if you have a Google account, you already have a YouTube account? All you need to do is activate it. YouTube is a very powerful social media and video broadcasting tool that, over the years, has risen to be considered the #2 search engine next to Google. This means that people actually go to YouTube to look things up—to find answers to questions they have, to watch how to do something, to be entertained, or for general knowledge or news. Having a presence on YouTube is one of the easiest ways to become found on the Internet because Google displays videos toward the top of search results. If you are interested, you might also want to look into YouTube's Live option or Creator Studio as well as a favorite of some, Google Hangouts. For the purpose of this book we will focus on creating your channel, which you can then organize with your training videos or for marketing through the Playlist feature.

Here's how to set up your account so that you can either post pre-recorded video or upload live broadcasting video recordings when you are off the air.

1. Set up an account at YouTube.com. Click the red Create Account if you do not already have one. You will be prompted

to connect to a Google account, which, if you are not already using one specifically for business, can be created just for this purpose.

2. When done registering, click under your username or on the left sidebar to access your Channel.

3. Customize your channel to match the colors of what you might choose for your personal branding. Canva.com offers a nice template for creating the top artwork. Edit the landing page to include links to your website, other social channels and your contact information.

4. Fill out your personal YouTube channel description completely as this will appear on your account as the channel host. Include information about your business and any relevant links.

5. Include your headshot as the account profile image. As with other social media sites, I do not recommend that you use a logo or product picture as that is too impersonal.

6. If you're shy on camera, consider making a video by using a screen recording such as Camtasia, Screenflow, or Screencaster, and show computer activity or a slide presentation while you speak.

7. Create helpful videos, how-to tutorials, or recorded screen presentations about working from home, succeeding at direct sales, or sharing general business tips. These videos need only be one or two minutes long. If you are giving out purely helpful advice, you will gain subscribers and shares. In the description of each video, complete a paragraph explaining what you talked about but then also include "boilerplate" content about you, your business and how to

contact you. This way those who were really impacted by your video can find out more.

8. If you create training videos you would prefer to keep private, just mark them as Unlisted and they will not go out to the news feed or subscribers and will not be findable in the searches. However, they can be accessed by anyone with the link. Then either share the link in your private Facebook Group, or email, text or message it to your team.

9. Include a call to action at the end of your videos, either as a graphics panel or verbally asking them to take action. If this is a team training, give them a job to do related to what you discussed in the training. If this is a marketing video, ask your viewers to take the next step, such as contacting you, commenting on the video or visiting your website.

10. Add thorough descriptions for each video and include keyword "tags" where prompted. I also like to include a made-up "tag" that no one else would use. Since YouTube finds similar videos to suggest when your viewers are done watching a video, this unique tag will help ensure it suggests your own video if they all include this tag.

11. Be social on YouTube. When signed into your account, watch other videos on related topics to yours (but not direct competitors) and leave comments or video responses to gain exposure from viewers in a similar market or who serve a similar demographic. Favorite other videos, or add them to your playlist of non-competing channels that provide good information. Again, you will become a resource for others this way.

12. Integrate your YouTube channel with your other online presence platforms—add a button that connects to your

channel on your team blog if you have one, let your customers know they can find you on YouTube, and share your videos on your social media sites.

13. Invite your distributors to subscribe to your YouTube channel (email the link or share it on social media sites) and to share appropriate videos to their own networks. If they create their own YouTube channels, encourage them to "favorite" the company's videos or add them to a playlist so they will display on their channel.

A note about posting pre-recorded video on Facebook: If you are using YouTube to host your videos, it is best to upload the video directly to Facebook instead of simply sharing the YouTube link. This is true for both marketing videos on your Business Page or training videos in your group. Videos simply display better when uploaded directly. When you post a YouTube link, it is as if you are sharing a website link and you will only receive a small thumbnail. It is less eye catching. Furthermore, on your Facebook Business Page, if you enable the Videos tab, you can select one video to be a larger Featured Video. The videos appearing on this tab are only videos that you have uploaded directly to Facebook (not YouTube video links) so try your hand at creating your own quick video talking about the benefits of your business opportunity to be shown as your featured video.

Live Broadcasting via Facebook Live

Live video broadcasting for the average person (vs. news stations!) has been popular for a while using desktop computer-based tools but increased in use after mobile apps like Meerkat and Periscope were created. The desktop-based live broadcasting was a bit intimidating for most individuals. However, when the ability to broadcast video live from your phone came out, people were all over it! Periscope, in particular, got people opening up to the idea of just pointing their phone at their faces and starting to talk! Periscope is very social and the comments and "hearts" were addicting to a lot of people. The problem was, though, that most of the viewers on Periscope are other Periscope users, which tended to be those who were a little more tech-savvy "first adopters," and not necessarily the general public. Periscope had a lot of promise, and if you are using it and have a following there, I would not necessarily give it up. But when Facebook decided to "copy" them, they were very successful if only because that's where most of the people are! Now you have a way to "go live" and your friends can immediately join in and watch. When it's public, such as on a Business Page, their friends can join in, too, and their friends, and their friends, and so on. It really has been a boon for individuals and businesses!

Something that live broadcasting offers more than pre-recorded video is the sense that you are real and relatable. If done well, it is unscripted and genuine, and the audience really gets a sense of what you know, who you are, and how much you care. It is as if you are stopping in to say hi and have a chat face to face. It really feels more personal and interactive. But just as with live television, it can also be and feel very risky! Anything can go wrong and your audience is watching! With pre-recorded video, if something goes wrong with the technology you can fix it by editing later, or scrapping the video and starting over—not so with live broadcasting! For this reason it's extra important to be prepared as I mentioned above, and to practice a bit to prevent any glitches. At the end of the day, even if you do have some trouble, your audience will understand, but why not do what you can to make things go smoothly? Here's how to use Facebook Live — either for training within your team group, for sales or opportunity events in a Facebook Event or for marketing in general on your Business Page.

1. It's always best to invite people or let them know in advance when you will be going live. Do this through a post or with the other invitation methods I mentioned above. This will help increase your attendance. Just before you go on, post another comment on that thread so they get a notification that way, too. If you have already instructed your team to get notifications in your group, and this is for a training, Facebook will notify them as well.

2. I recommend you start setting up for your video at least five or ten minutes in advance so you can adjust the settings and go live right at the time you said you would. Have a drink nearby, your outline, your device charged up or a spare charger nearby. I even like to have a small hand mirror and powder or brush nearby so I can touch up just before. Be 100 percent ready!

3. When you first click the Live Video button to start a broadcast, you may need to click the button to turn the camera to be facing you. It should stay there by default for future broadcasts.

4. Next, I recommend you putting your phone in "landscape" mode which is the "long way" so there is a larger screen showing, rather than the vertical orientation. When I was teaching school, we used to call this the "hot dog" way vs. the "hamburger" way! The video shows up nicely and it is more pleasing to the eye. It is said that if you position yourself not in the center but just off to the right a little, people

stay more engaged and feel more comfortable. You will know your orientation is set up correctly because your name will be across the bottom. Of course sometimes it's more comfortable or convenient to stay in the portrait position and that is fine too. Most people are used to looking at live video "squares" and won't notice.

5. Next, where it says "Describe your live video..." type in an engaging title for your video. You will be able to edit this later or add an additional caption, but telling others what the broadcast is about will help make sure they click to watch it.

6. At the top right, next to the button to turn the video toward you, you will see a "magic wand" button to adjust the settings. You can do this before you broadcast. There are buttons for filters that might make the coloring of your video better, or might not. The button that looks like a set of tools has the option to flip horizontally because, by default, your video will be a mirror image. So if there is anything you would be holding up with words such as a book or flier, it would appear to be backwards. Use the Horizontal Flip button in the tools to get it to appear correctly. On that same tools setting, there is also a Brightness button that can correct the lighting if need be. Tap it once or twice for a boost. Also find the mask and pencil buttons, which allow you to add funny masks to your face or to write or draw on your video. These may seem too silly for business, but they can be really fun during a team game or casual chat for team building! After you are done with the settings, click the X to go back to starting your video.

7. Click the Go Live button when you are ready! You will see the red Live button at the top.

8. You will be able to watch comments come in and address them at a set time or at the end. People watching will be able to "react" to your video by clicking on heart and thumbs-up symbols, which will seem to "fly" across the screen. These will all help increase your visibility if this is a public video.

9. When you feel your broadcast is complete, give them a "call to action" that encourages them to implement what you discussed. Then say goodbye and click the Finish button. You will then be shown your video and given the opportunity to trim it before posting it. This is handy if there were any glitches at the beginning or end that you would like edited out, but it isn't necessary. Next to the Trim button you will see the HD Upload On button and a download button. The download button will save the video to your camera roll, which will allow you to later upload it to YouTube if you wish.

10. Click Post when you are ready to post your replay. There will be a short time for processing before the video appears on your group or page, and then you can go back to edit the caption or add more information in the comments. If you are using Facebook on the desktop, you can also edit the title, add some category tags, download the video to your computer, or grab the code to embed the video on your team blog.

Ideas for Using Facebook Live

Here are some other ideas that leaders can use to integrate live streaming in their businesses in addition to training:

- **Online parties.** Demonstrate and carry out your party similarly to an in-home experience on a Business Page event.

- **Opportunity Events.** Invite your team to invite their prospects, who then ask questions about the business. Share the benefits of joining, some company history, and your "why stories." See my chapter on <u>Online Team Meetings and Rallies</u> for more ideas.

- **Monthly Recognition.** Go on screen to announce and celebrate your top achievers. Invite them to share how they met their goals in the comments.

- **Open Q/A.** Conduct a general "town hall" type show where customers and the public can ask questions about your product or opportunity.

- **Unboxing New Product.** When there's a new product launch, unbox your new stash live online! Invite team members to be there in the comments, and then everyone can share what they love most.

- **Demonstrate Product.** Teach people how to use your product. Have customers share what they have from your product line in the comments while you explain features/benefits and how-tos.

- **Work at Home Biz Chat.** Conduct a generic broadcast about working from home — strategies, tips, suggestions. Let others chime in through the comments or ask questions and learn more about your business via your link.

- **Hot Seat Coaching.** Have new team members come on to BeLive.tv to get some live coaching from you. Model how to coach new consultants while showing the support you offer.

- **Top Tips.** Have a list of lesser known tips and tricks for using your product. Invite others to comment and share their tips too.

- **Interview Industry Experts**. Using BeLive.tv, elevate your own reputation by hosting interviews with speakers, trainers and authors in the direct sales industry.

- **Interview Leaders**. Select leaders from your team or company and interview them about an area in which they excel, or a strategy they've used that works.

- **Book Talk.** Discuss a book that has helped you in your business and share your favorite parts.

- **Company Announcements.** Explain company announcements, contests, policy changes, and other news. Take questions in the comments and discuss or jot them down for future trainings.

- **Trivia Contests.** Play a trivia game with your team about your company/products. They answer in the comments and tally points for whoever answered first. Then do a giveaway for the winner with the most points. Get help with this or add them up later!

- **Fundraising Live-a-Thon.** If your company has a cause or charity it supports, have a show where you discuss that cause. Interview people affected by it and brainstorm ways to help, while encouraging purchases or donations.

- **Event Coverage.** Live stream your conference, retreats, summits and other events. Stop and interview people to ask what they've learned or have team members join in on their own phones.

Online Launch Parties

As a leader, when you bring on a new team member, helping them conduct a launch party is one of the ways that you can foster activity and success right away. Traditionally, launch parties are done locally and often the leader will either do the party for the new team member who has invited her network, in exchange for a portion of the commission, or she will simply teach her new team member the basics of how to do a show and the new representative will host her own party, introducing her friends and family to her new business.

An online launch party is a great supplement to an in-person launch party, though I do not recommend it as a replacement! Of course we want our new team members to introduce the products and opportunity to her local contacts. As a supplement, an online launch party allows her to also reach her long distance friends and family, and even generate interest among her online friends she may have never met in person.

When it comes to online launch parties, they can be done the same way as an offline launch party, but using a social media party, video streaming, or an online event. Some companies offer general launch party training, so check and see if there are guidelines you can follow and see how they could be adapted to an online launch party.

The purpose of a launch party is not so much to make sales or sponsor people, as it is to generate leads that will build your, and your new representative's, businesses. If you are in a party plan company, this means the goal is for your new team member to get bookings for either offline or online parties, and if you are in network marketing this means the goal is to create interest in your products and opportunity. In both cases you will want to have a built-in way to collect contact information so that your team member can follow-up.

I recommend that launch parties be held within the first two weeks of someone joining your team. By then they would have received materials from the company such as a starter kit, and the leads they get from the launch party can be used during their first qualifying period if your company offers some sort of "fast start" incentive. If you wait too long to hold the launch party, it may take too long to conduct the appointments or bookings that result from it and you may miss some incentive deadlines.

Whether you are helping your new consultant conduct her launch party or simply training her to do one, you will want to choose a platform. For launch parties I strongly recommend using a Facebook Business Page event because they are public, which makes it easier to get interest from non-friends or friends of friends. Also, it is a great way to get her new Business Page active right away, which teaches the algorithm that her page is important!

If she has not yet set up a Business Page on Facebook, that's okay! The launch party can be her inaugural activity. You could even set up a simple page for her, and then add her as an admin. She can fill in the information and personalize it on her own but that way she has an official Business Page ready to go, and the event for the launch party can be created within that page.

Launch Party How-To on a Facebook Business Page

Here is how I suggest launch parties be conducted on a Facebook Page event. Teach this to your team or do it along with them:

1. Set up the party in your website/back office if you have that functionality.

2. Decide on things you will be posting during the launch (see below) and save any images into a folder on your computer.

3. Gather and/or prepare any images or graphics you will want to use with your posts. If your company provides these, great! Set up a folder on the device you will be using live, and place the images there. If you need to create your own images (following your company guidelines) you might want to try a tool such as <u>Canva.com</u> or <u>PicMonkey.com</u> which allow you to add words to backgrounds or images if needed. For example, you may want to create a post that says "Welcome!" or "Thank You For Coming!" See the section on Posts below for more ideas of what you might need.

4. Create a list of everyone you would like to invite. With a regular online party, less is more, but with a launch party I recommend inviting everyone you know!

5. Prepare your "Why" story. This is a detailed story explaining why you joined your company and the difference it is (or will be) making for you or your family. It is a good idea to include emotional elements or "heart tugs" throughout your story so that others can relate and start to see how the business can make a difference for them, too. Write this out and/or prepare a video talking about it.

6. Set your Launch Party goal. Remember that the main objective is to get leads with contact information so that you can start filling your pipeline for gaining new sales, new team members and new party bookings if you are in a party plan company. Ask yourself how many contacts would you like from this? How many requests for information about the income opportunity? How many party bookings? If you have a sample request system, how many of those do you want?

7. Prepare your Facebook Event. For the purposes of this book, I am going to explain below how to do this on a Facebook Business Page Event, even though this could also be done using other platforms.

Steps to Prepare Your Event

1. Visit the Business Page and find the Events tab under the More button just under the cover image. Click on Create Event.

2. Set the Date. I recommend about one week out.

3. Write your Description. Explain that you are excited to be launching your business and would love to tell people all about it. Also include your replicated website link if you have one, in case anyone wants to look up more infor-

mation in advance. You can also include your link in the "Tickets" box, which is clickable once the event is submitted.

Here is an example, though I suggest you put it into your own words and maybe shorten it a bit. I included everything since I am one of those detail people!

I just started a new business venture as an Independent _____ Consultant and am so excited! To get my business started, I will be holding an online Launch Party right here on Facebook!

My Launch Party will be held live on _____(date/time) and last about _____ (choose length, usually 30-60 minutes). You can Join the event any time – watch for some fun pre-party posts!

During the Launch Party I will share information about my new business and answer any questions you might have. I will be posting lots of pictures so be sure to visit this event page during the party and refresh the Discussion tab often to get the newest posts! You are going to love _____(company name) as much as I do, I am sure!

If you want a sneak peek or decide to try _____ (company) yourself here's how you do that:

Go to my launch party website: bitly.com/karensnewbiz.

I am looking for Hosts for either in-person _____(company) Parties or online Facebook Parties. If you would like to have a fun party with your friends, too, please message me on this page so we can find a day that works!

If you like the idea of having your OWN _____ (company name) business, let's talk! I am looking for help sharing _____ (company name) all around the US and Canada. If this interests you, message me and I can send you some more information!

Look around and let me know what you think! I am especially interested in someone booking their OWN _____ (company name) party or joining my team, doing what I do! If either of those interest you, let me know right away and I can send you some more information!

If you decide to purchase something, you can do that here: bit-ly.com/karensparty.

Thank you for the support!! Feel free to message me or post within the event if you have any questions!

Karen Clark, NEW Independent _____ Consultant :)

4. Upload a picture for the banner at the top, or use the one Facebook includes.

5. Set up a few posts in advance so that there is some information for the early birds to browse. I recommend pre-loading your event with any of the detailed information about your business or opportunity that you may not have time to cover during the event. This will give those who are more detail-oriented more information, and you can also refer back to the posts (or tag someone in them) if questions arise.

6. Note that we are not yet inviting people to the event. It is important that you first get everything set up and then personally invite them. See below for more information about inviting guests.

7. I like setting up a short-URL for the event page URL itself since it is often quite long. You can use this shorter web address in your personalized messages or invitations. Go to the top of your browser while on the event page and highlight and copy the full URL of the event. Then go to a

shortener such as bitly.com and paste it in to get a shorter link. You can even customize your short link so it is something like bitly.com/karensnewbiz. I like Bitly because, if you sign up for a free account, it will give you statistics on how many clicks your link received. If you also have a special link in your back office to the party ordering page, you may want to create a short link for that as well to make things easier and also to be able to track clicks.

8. If you do not have a built-in contact page on your company-replicated website that gathers contact information and interest level, set up a form to collect this information yourself using something like forms.google.com. I recommend you request their name, email, phone number. In addition, set up checkboxes where they can select things they are interested in, such as purchasing products, scheduling an in-home demonstration, scheduling an online sales party, information about the income opportunity, and any other offers you may have. If possible, also add a text box asking them for any additional comments. You will be using the submission of these forms as not only a way to gather leads. but as a way to pick a random winner for your door prize drawing. You may want to set up another Bitly short URL for this form as well.

9. Decide on and prepare for mailing small prizes for your door prize and possibly a game. Keep it simple—no need to break the bank. Most people appreciate the fun of winning and aren't concerned with the value of the prize. It could be a small sample or even a $5 credit or rebate on their next order.

10. Invite your guests. This can be done through email, private message, texting or phone call. Yes, even though it is a "virtual" event, phone calls are great! You may get their voicemail, but it gives you an opportunity to personally invite them in a way that conveys how excited you are! Whenever possible, personalize your invitation to something you know that person would be interested in whether it is a certain product line, or gathering friends together for a "girls night out," or a way for them to pay for that kitchen remodel they've been wanting. Letting them know you were thinking of them feels great. As I mentioned above, you just can't over-invite for a launch party. The more people who attend the party, the better kickoff you will have for your business! When you send them the personal message, or follow up by email, give them the shortened event link you created earlier. Anyone who says they are "Going" or "Interested/Maybe" on a Facebook event will get a reminder before the event and will get notifications of any posts in the event. This is what makes a Facebook Event a great place to hold an online launch party!

11. Once someone says Yes or Maybe to your invitation, go ahead and use the built-in Invite button on the event page if they had not yet clicked the link you sent them to join the event.

12. Also, go to the event page and click the Share Event button to share the event to your personal Facebook timeline. This will help catch anyone who may not have received a personal invitation or who may not have opened it yet. If you mark this message as Public, then you also have an opportunity to have that post be seen by friends of friends who may like or comment on it.

13. If you are a member of any Facebook Groups that allow you to promote your business, share the online launch party information and link there, too! For this type of event, it is okay to invite total strangers. And you never know who may be looking for a new opportunity. In the Facebook Group search, you will find many of these groups by searching on topics such as "direct sales" or "direct selling."

14. Try some offline marketing, too! You could even create a flier about your new business launch and put it out at your or your spouse's workplace, the teacher's lunchroom at your child's school, or on the church bulletin board.

15. Now it is time to start posting! Once your invitations have gone out and you start having people join the event page, you can start posting something each day leading up to the event. Then, during the live event, I recommend every five minutes or so—keep it to about a half hour total. This means you will have only six "live" posts during the party time, including your lead collection/door prize, so it is important to plan ahead based on your goals. Below are some suggestions of ideas for posts. Decide which of these might be posted during the days leading up to the event, and which you might want to post during the live event. Some can even be posted in the two or three days after the event.

Here's a tip: You can include multiple images in ONE post so it "counts" as one post but shows several products. Note that it is not necessary to show them everything! I recommend picking YOUR favorite items. They can always see more when they visit your website. You can also post about one thing, but then add more images as comments on that post. This works great, especially if someone asks a specific question. Have your image collection ready to go or your website open in another window so you can easily direct people to the right place.

Launch Party Post Ideas

- What is _____? (company). Give some background on the company, its mission or founder's story.

- Introducing _____ (product line or category). Share some posts about the various product lines you carry. This is a good place to post a multi-image post or share the link to a Facebook album you've set up.

- Welcome post. Ask them to like the post to "check in" or comment with where they are from or how they know you. You can also get creative and ask another question, either silly and random, or pertaining to your topic. The idea is to get everyone interacting.

- Share your "Why" story or video.

- Share any company testimonials about the products or business. Be sure not to make any health or income claims that would be non-compliant.

- Share any seasonal or monthly specials or featured products and why you love them.

- If your company has any additional services such as a pre-ferred customer program or a monthly delivery box, share information about that.

- If your product requires any kind of how-to or demonstration, share a video or images with that information.

- Post about how one might earn discounts or free product, such as by booking a party, and the benefits of doing that.

- Post about the income opportunity and that you are looking for a buddy to do the business with. This could also be an "Ask Me About My Job" game where they ask questions about your income opportunity and you choose a random winner for a prize.

- Announce your door prize drawing and give them the link to your entry form. Give them a few minutes to fill it out and then at the very end you will announce the winner in the comments.

- Any questions? Give them a chance to explore things you may not have brought up, and answer their questions in the comments.

- Thank you post to thank anyone who ordered, signed up or booked a party.

- Goodbye! Let them know you will be following up with them and if there were any orders you will be placing them on _____ date (I recommend within 48 hours).

- Post-party, you might wish to post a few daily things such as inviting them to like your Business Page if they haven't already, or asking them to share your page with a friend. You might also want to thank any hosts who booked parties, and welcome new team members who signed up.

After your event, it is critical that you follow-up with each person, ideally based on the contact form she used for her door prize drawing. You can use these calls to thank them for their orders, or for booking, or to see if they had any questions, or invite them to book a party or consider doing this business too.

If you have mailing addresses, it is always nice to mail a thank you as well!

If you are training your team to conduct launch parties for their new team members, it is critical that you ensure that the new consultants follow up! This is where the relationship can be solidified with their new customers and future hosts. They may even find that they are able to bring someone else into the business when they take the time to really connect with each person.

If any orders were placed, you can go back to the event page (it will be on your Business Page's event tab, but under Past Events) and see if anyone has questions. Ask how they like their orders. Post any useful instructions or reminders that would help them have a great experience.

Tips from the Trenches

Connie Ignacio

When I started in direct sales my only intention was to be a "kit snatcher." I'm very shy, socially awkward, an introvert, and I suffer from severe social anxiety — so bad to the point I had my groceries delivered to my house. I'm embarrassed to say I didn't even know what direct sales was. I just knew my friend on Facebook was talking about a mascara I just had to try....Little did I know I was just introduced to a whole new way of life. And as Princess Jasmine would say, "A whole new world, a hundred thousand things to see, I'm like a shooting star, I've come so far, I can't go back to where I used to be." After trying the mascara, I just had to try more products, so I got the Presenters kit.

In my first month I promoted three times and earned my company's fast start program in a third of the time allotted. Within three months I advanced to the first level of leadership. LEADER, WHAT?!? I'm not a leader. I'm a follower. At this point I had to decide, am I going to man up and take control of my life, or am I going to continue to let it take control of me? So I took the reins and held on tight! In 16 months I made it to the top one percent of my company. This made me a firm believer that leaders are made, not born.

I became a corporate event junkie — a sponge for knowledge. If there was a training, I was there. Being surrounded by like-minded individuals was so empowering, so I took that and ran with it. How could I recreate these for my team? I knew I wanted to do something monthly, and I knew I wanted to make it engaging. I found that the better relationships teammates had with one another, the better they did with their businesses. My local meetings were a huge hit, but with a team spread across the US and growing internationally, I knew there had to be another way. So I tried different things and found what works.

Here are my top three favorite ways for recreating events for my team: 1.) monthly meet-ups via video conferencing 2.) a book club concentrated solely on personal or business development and 3.) promotional chats where teammates going for the same company promotion are put into a group chat via Facebook Messenger and are given the tools to be successful in ways specific to the promotion they are going for.

Video Conferencing

These are monthly meet-ups via video conference. There are a few different programs for this—my favorite is Zoom.us. It's free, but you have the option to upgrade for longer meeting times or bigger audiences. Plus, these can be recorded for those who aren't able to make it on live. With that said, I encourage making it live by offering an incentive for attending—some sort of giveaway. When the team joins live they have a better chance of connecting and building relationships, and it also gives them the option to be heard. I love the video conference aspect of these meetings because it really allows faces from all over to connect. Nothing beats being able to see and hear someone speak.

I schedule these meet-ups to take place at the same time and the same place each month. I found the first Thursday of the month at 5:00 p.m. PST works great. By having them on consistent days and times, everyone knows that unless they hear otherwise they can rely on the fact that the first Thursday of the month at 5:00 p.m. we will be doing a meet-up. At the beginning of the month we all start fresh; we are ready to run. I found this time of the month is also when attention is the highest. My goal is to keep the training part to around 30 minutes and to always end the session with a Q&A.

"One of the most important leadership lessons is realizing you're not the most important or the most intelligent person in the room at all times."
— Mario Batali

I ask one to three teammates to speak on a topic they are really doing well in. I have them speak about things like: organization, sales, sponsoring, time management, creating loyal customers, being coachable, being consistent, personal development — just to name a few. Asking ladies at all levels of the company to help train allows me to start building up their leadership qualities. It gives them confidence, and makes them feel empowered and validated that what they are doing is on the right track. Reproduction is the fastest road to success. I've also asked other leaders to pop in and share some motivating words. I close the meet-ups with tips on working their businesses, depending on the season or what is going on in the company, such as if there is a new product launch or something else going on.

Since starting these monthly meet-ups, I have noticed my team getting closer, they are feeling more prepared to take on their businesses, they are selling more, they are sponsoring more, and best of all, they are feeling confident! This is what a few have said about these online events:

"I love our Zooms. I always feel connected and motivated afterwards!"
— Kristen Vauiso

"I always take away notes when we have our speakers"
— Heather Womack

TEAM Book Club

My favorite thing about this industry is the person you become. Growing your knowledge is the quickest way to grow your paycheck, so I really stress the importance of personal development. To encourage this, I started a book club. It all takes place in a Facebook Group. I post in my team group which book we will be reading and the link to the book club group. Those interested in reading it with us can add themselves to the book club group. I have tried a few different methods

177

for staying on track and my favorite has become chapter discussions. After each chapter, I post a few questions related to that chapter and ask the group to share their biggest takeaways. The beauty of doing it this way is that no matter what your schedule or lifestyle is, you can go at your own pace.

Once the book is completed, we as a group pick a new book. Again, it gets posted in the main team group page and we repeat the process with chapter discussions. Any book related to personal or business development is considered when we are making the selection. My team has really loved this; it gives them the opportunity to really work on themselves and it becomes a sense of meditation for some.

Promotional Chat Groups

My latest idea, and probably my most successful and beneficial one, is Facebook Group chats. I call them "RUNNERS groups." There is a group for each promotional level in the company including one for New Presenters. In my company, our levels are based on colors. When the group chat is created, the photo relates to the color they are going for, as well as the name.

Everyone who is ready to run for that promotion is added to this group chat. After introductions, everyone is assigned a pacing partner. I have a few "leaders in training" help me monitor these groups and make sure the environment remains motivating, uplifting and encouraging.

Every so often a task is given that is based on the promotion they are going for. For example, an entry-level promotion task might be following three people that inspire you. I give them a list of some of my favorites and have them share a screen shot when they have completed this. Another task would be making sure your profile picture is of your pretty smiling face, and your banner should be something that inspires you and makes you happy.

Being a part of the first direct sales company to market and sell almost exclusively through the use of social media, our Facebook profiles become the faces of our businesses. We are now in the business of growing our network and when someone new visits a team member's Facebook profile, the first thing they see is a profile picture and cover photo. That's why you want it to be positive, happy and uplifting.

Another favorite task is quizzing each level on what the requirements are for the promotion they are going for, then asking for different ideas on how they can achieve that promotion. Then I ask them what is one thing they will each do today toward that goal.

For promotions leading up to leadership levels, I have them check in on members of their team who have been added to the entry level runner groups and make sure they are happy with their pacing partners. I also teach them how to road map and plan their month, and how they can help their team do the same. This helps break down that large goal into daily goals and this really helps them to stay on track.

Between monthly meet-ups via video conferencing, the team book club and the promotional group chats, all bases are covered. These are all very duplicable methods of training and as a result, every teammate is set up for success. The power of duplication is to have MORE in life – MORE time and MORE money!

Connie Ignacio
Independent Younique Exclusive Presenter
doesyourmakeupdothis.com

Imee Birkett

I use Facebook Groups, Facebook Messenger and Zoom to train and support our teams. When we have a health transformation challenge, we set up a Facebook Group so that participants can ask questions, get nutrition and fitness tips, recipes, support and motivation. They feel part of a wonderful and supportive community as they journey to better their health. It is exciting to see people cheer each other on as they share the challenges they overcome, successes they achieve and their "Before" and "After" pictures.

We also have a Facebook Group for team members who are building their Isagenix business. Here we update the group on promotions, contests and product offerings. In addition, we share trainings on our various duplicable systems. We encourage team members to ask questions and share insights, strategies and inspiration. We also recognize rank advancements and celebrate successes in this group. We use this group to empower each other to grow, gain confidence, and become better leaders.

We use Facebook Messenger as a quicker way to communicate with team members. I find that this is a more effective way to disseminate timely information and important announcements or to get immediate responses or feedback from others. For instance, if a new team member has set an appointment with a candidate and needs a leader to do a three-way call with her, then she can send a group message and someone who can help her can respond right away.

Lastly, we use Zoom meetings to educate people who are interested in our health solutions and financial opportunity. We also use them to stay connected with the team, train and learn, and celebrate each other. I love using Zoom as it is convenient, simple to use, and it allows us to meet "face to face" with team members around the world.

Imee Birkett
Independent Isagenix Executive
imeebirkett.com

Jennifer Harmon

As a Corporate Advisor, I've been working with companies looking to advance their virtual offerings to those in direct sales. One that I'm over the moon excited about is a virtual event tool through TurnKey Social. This tool marries the value of video presentation with e-commerce blended with just-in-time purchasing. Think QVC with bonus features for direct sellers. It's so impactful! You can stream it live or through replay. As you promote a product on video, the product shows up at the bottom of the video screen with an Add to Cart feature. The best thing is, you can use it as a stand-alone, or invite your entire downline to participate. Each person is given a unique link that ties in any purchases or sign-ups back to the person who invited them! Think how amazing this tool is for online opportunity events!

Several companies are now using TurnKey Social's newest tool and are seeing an increase in their online sales and sign-ups. TurnKey Social currently works with Facebook, Twitter, Instagram, LinkedIn and Google+. As we expand globally, we will add Vine, Weibo, and others as we have demand. Most virtual presentation platforms allow you to take the customer or prospect to the point of being interested, but without a mechanism to close the sale or to sign someone who is interested. With TurnKey, we can take the customer all the way to the close. Leaders I work with love that they have a duplicable way to succeed with online sales, sponsoring, on-boarding and training.

Jennifer Harmon
Corporate Business Development Advisor
linkedin.com/in/jennifer-l-harmon

Jennifer Johnson

Leaders have had amazing results using CinchShare, noting an increase in sales, recruits and team promotions, as well as a boost in overall morale! CinchShare is social media marketing software that saves leaders in direct sales a ton of time so they can focus on other projects and spend those quality moments with their families while maintaining their presence online.

CinchShare's unique features allow them to easily manage their daily multiple tasks: providing the necessary support and training for their teams, keeping their Business Pages updated, timelines and Facebook parties consistent and planning ahead for a stress-free, productive month by being able to engage and be present for their team, instead of worrying about posting manually every day.

I'm a busy mom of four. Truth be told, CinchShare wasn't originally meant to be used by anyone but me. My husband Joel just happens to be a programming genius so I asked him to whip up a program for me. Pretty amazing hubby, right? I'm a lucky woman! (Don't tell him I said that lol.) After using the software for a couple weeks, I shared it with my upline, Heili, who was blown away, and then my downline and company—everyone loved it! News kept spreading by word of mouth and Joel and I realized that we could help so many who work online.

The CinchShare Team really wants to help every direct seller and small business owner have a life and be successful, which is why we strive to be a valuable tool that simplifies social media marketing. We want you to be able to have a life offline while still maintaining a presence online and help you do that without sacrificing your business or family. No one should ever have to choose between the two!

Jennifer Johnson
CinchShare Founder and CEO
cinchshare.com

Jennifer Quisenberry

Using Collaborative Boards on Pinterest to Grow Your Business

Pinterest is one of the greatest tools available to grow your business. A lot of people think of Pinterest as a social network. Instead, think of it as a search engine for visual content — a visual search engine that lends itself to introducing others to your content in a fun and easily searchable format.

An often-overlooked feature on Pinterest is collaborative or group boards. Collaborative boards are exactly what they sound like — rather than hosting pins from a single user, a collaborative board hosts pins from multiple users.

To tell if a board is collaborative, open the board and look at the top right section. A collaborative board will display multiple users' avatars. Some collaborative boards have so many guest pinners contributing that only three avatars will show, and you will need to open a dropdown menu to see the full list of contributors. You can find examples of collaborative boards on my Pinterest profile, pinterest.com/theawesomemuse.

What are the benefits of hosting or participating in a collaborative board?

- *Convenience. Collaborative boards show up on the user profile of each person pinning to that board. For example, if you have a collaborative board for your team, whatever you pin to that board will automatically show up on each member's user profile AND in their feed, unless you have marked the board as private. That's a great way to disseminate visual information to your team.*

- *Growth. When someone elects to follow you and all of your boards, this person will now be following the group board too.*

Your pins will be seen by more people, some of whom may opt to view your personal pins as well.

- **Content Activity.** *Collaborative boards make it easy to share content more frequently. Pinterest profiles thrive when their contributors post new pins daily. When you have a group of people regularly posting content to a board, it's a lot easier to post every day throughout the day. Your profile becomes more robust, and thus more enticing to those who follow you.*

- **Increase Your Reach.** *Group boards increase the number of likes and re-pins you get because the content is exposed to more people. This can translate to more traffic to your site, which has the potential to lead to more customers. For example, let's say you have 200 followers and there are 9 more contributors to the board who have 200 followers each. If all of those people follow the collaborative board, your pins may show up in the feeds of as many as 2,000 people.*

How do you create a collaborative board?
The good news is, it's really easy. Here are the steps you need to do so:
1. *Go to your Pinterest user profile and either select or create a board you would like to become a group board.*

2. *On the board's top right, you will see a plus (+) sign. Click the plus sign.*

3. *You will then be prompted to select or search for someone's username or to add their email address.*

4. *The people you invite will receive the invitation via direct message in their Pinterest messages (and possibly an email depending on how they have configured their settings). They will be able to opt-in to participate in the group board. It's that simple.*

You always want to ask permission to add people to a collaborative board prior to issuing the invitation. They may not know what it is and ignore the invitation, or they may not be interested in participating.

What are some ways to use a collaborative board on Pinterest to boost your business?

- *Team communication*

- *Sharing user-generated content for product launches and increasing reach and awareness*

- *Seasonal gift ideas*

- *Customer education*

- *Connect with different direct sellers to promote multiple shopping opportunities*

- *Establish yourself as an authority on your subject*

- *Host multi-consultant sales*

Most collaborative boards have rules for participation. You will want to establish rules or guidelines for the collaborative boards you create. For example, I would suggest that you only allow pins that are: vertical, visually stunning, images you have created yourself or have permission to use, in focus, and on brand.

Most collaborative boards also limit the number of pins someone can add per day. Sharing three pins per contributor per day is a great practice. Most board owners require that you re-pin two pins from the board for each pin you add to it in order to keep the board healthy. If a pin doesn't fit in with the spirit of the board, the board owner can easily delete it. Have a great time pinning on collaborative boards on Pinterest. Be sure to let me know how your boards are growing!

Jennifer Quisenberry
The Awesome Muse, Editor-in-Chief

theawesomemuse.com

Kim Chapman

I wanted to share how I promote myself and my brand online through Facebook posting. The posting style that I'll be presenting, inspired by Kristine Weyher, works because it engages your audience and doesn't make them feel like you're constantly advertising to them. This is essential to your business when building online through Facebook. Network marketing doesn't have to be face-to-face, but it does have to be heart-to-heart — connecting is vital.

Post #1 — Post this type of post EVERY day

Post something personal (non-brand related) on your page each day. This post should include a picture to make it interesting and engaging. What is most exciting in your life today? Your kids, your garden, your pets? Are you going somewhere fun? Take a picture of yourself there and write something cute! Are you stuck in traffic and pondering deep thoughts? Take a picture of the traffic and tell your audience what's on your mind. Be creative, be fun, BE POSITIVE, and pull your audience in!

Post #2 — Post this type of post EVERY day

Stop selling and pitching to people and start ENGAGING them with your posting! When I first started sharing the love and passion I have for my product, I had a lot of people tell me that others on Facebook selling things annoyed them like crazy, but that they loved that I was just sharing my excitement with them and not always trying to sell and get the next customer! Be sure to have this post be about either:

- *A personal difference your product has made in your life or the life of a family member or friend*

- *How you use one of your brand's products in your everyday life*

Post #3 — Post this type of post at least twice a week

I want you to post something that is going to get you a LOT of comments and likes that are from PEOPLE (in contrast to people commenting from their Business Pages). This is especially important because Facebook's algorithms will show your brand-related posts to people simply because they interacted with this kind of post. This is a tricky one, but it's important to keep your audience engaged in your life and on your page. Asking questions to elicit audience response is key. Here are some examples of Post #3:

- *"Pay off the Mortgage or Invest?"*

- *"Beach or Mountains?"*

- *Post a picture of 2-4 things and ask friends to choose one.*

DID YOU KNOW that when you receive comments under a post, it becomes more likely to be shown in your friends' news feeds? You want your posts to be in your friends' news feeds. You MUST engage your audience!

After I build a rapport with someone by commenting back and forth on each other's posts, I reach out to them through private messaging and invite them to look at my brand. If they accept, I send them a "Guest Profile" using a software system called Zenplify. I gather information through this system so I can better center our private conversation around their needs. The system has follow-up steps integrated into it as well. In this field, the gold mine is in the follow-up.

Sharing ourselves openly through our personal Facebook profiles makes us more relatable, and I've found that people open up quicker and are less guarded because of this personal style of posting.

Kim Chapman

Independent Ambassador, Plexus WorldWide

shopmyplexus.com/wellnesscoachkim

Laurie Wright

A few months ago I started using Hootsuite, which is a scheduling website, to post to Instagram and to my team Facebook group. I use only the free version, which has been terrific for me and my current needs. I also have a closed Facebook group of customers, but I found the automated posts were not received well.

I started by downloading free graphics related to the days of the week. Quotes, jokes, and funny pictures all went into my file so that I had many to choose from each week. I sit down for an hour or so at a time and schedule team posts for about a month! It's amazingly simple and efficient.

I am reaching out to my team to motivate them, inform them or make them laugh EVERY DAY, which has increased the involvement on our team page drastically. If I didn't use this type of scheduler, I would not likely make the time to consistently post every day. It has improved my team communication, our feeling of camaraderie, and my efficiency as a leader.

Laurie Wright
Director with Thirty-One Gifts Canada
mybaglady.ca

Lisa Muth

I am a military spouse and we move often. With that, my team is broadly spread around the US. I am using Zoom and Facebook Live for team trainings. Zoom is an online video conferencing platform that you can use on your computer or your smart phone. It is like a call-in teleconference with the added feature of video! It is offered in both a free and a paid version.

As a leader, Zoom offers me the ability to have face-to-face contact with my long distance team and I am able see and feel their expressions and emotions through the conference. This has helped me to keep the lines of communication open with my team. In addition, Zoom brings the team together in one space. This app has been so helpful for my monthly meetings as well as my one-on-one trainings. Attendees on Zoom have the option to join by video through the app, or they can call in from their phone. It also allows me to screen share, mute, and save the conference for repurposing. Every direct sales leader needs Zoom in their tool box.

I am working really diligently on mindset with my team and what that can look like for them in their businesses, primarily through professional development to help them grow. I am using a system that Gale Bates teaches called Calendar Girls, where I reward my team members when they reach certain milestones in the month. I promote these on my Team Facebook group. I also have a Rock Star of the Month where I personally send post cards to the Top Two in sales along with an extra goodie from me, and of course they are highlighted in the team newsletter and on our team group page.

I reward and recognize small milestones too, like stepping out of their comfort zone for instance. For some, that is a huge, huge step. I am sure that it is common industry-wide to recognize the top, but there are some people on the team who may not hit the top levels in sales that are also special and amazing, and I want to make sure they know that.

Lisa Muth

Keep Me Safe Organics Advocate

lisamuth.com

facebook.com/cleanlivingwithlisamuth

Melissa Fietsam

Four Tips to Uncomplicate Your Leadership Role in Direct Sales

1. **Lead From the Front.** *You cannot expect your team to do things YOU are not doing. So lead from the front! Set goals in your own business and SHOW your team what you're doing! You should be posting a minimum of TWO times a day in your team page. What kinds of things?*

   - *Company updates*

   - *Company incentives*

   - *Resources*

   - *Trainings*

   - *And what YOU are doing in your business.*

   It's really quite easy to lead from the front when you are actually working everyday. Making hostess packets? Post a picture on your team page! Just had a recruiting conversation? Snap a pic and post it to your team. Give them the WORDS. And show them you're getting results because you're working.

2. **Trainings Don't Have to be Hard.** *In fact, they don't have to be from YOU at all! Do you know how many trainings are already out there? You don't have to come up with the trainings; it's simply your job to make sure they have access to them!*

   Find people who inspire you. Follow them on Facebook and on their blogs. Google is your best friend!

   And here's a couple of sites that have trainings and tips already laid out for you to SHARE with your team!

   Cinchshare: Go to the events tab link here and you can find dozens of trainings on any topic you can think of. Those events can be shared, and your team can go back through all of that great information at ANY TIME! And you know what? They hold WEEKLY live Facebook trainings from experts in the field. So you can invite your team to a new training every single week! When I realized this, it was a huge relief to me. I don't have to come up with all of that on my own!

Cinchshare Events Tab: facebook.com/pg/CinchShare/events

Cinch Socials: This is a Facebook page with nothing but direct sales tips. Go over and LIKE and FOLLOW the page and you can share a tip daily on your team page. EASY PEEZY!

Cinch Socials Page: facebook.com/CinchSocials

3. ***Keep It Positive and Set the Pace.*** *Set the TONE for your team. Don't know where to start? Use the description on your team page to set the expectation for the team. Have it be a place to encourage and lift each other up, to share ideas and celebrate your team members. Do they KNOW what you want? Have you ever told them your vision for your team? It's kind of important.*

Then set the rules. At the beginning of every month, I post the same post. It talks about the rules of the page. No complaining, no selling, and be nice. That's the gist of it. But it's long and detailed and I give them instructions on how to word their feelings if they are frustrated, and how to use the chain of contact in a message to their upline to actually vent those frustrations privately and get results. They don't know if you don't TELL them.

And third, you better STICK TO IT. No excuses. Delete any posts that violate this and send a personal, thoughtful and positive message to anyone who goes against that. You might get some resistance at first, but after that, you will have the positive, work-

ing environment you crave. And your team members will be happy you did it! There is NO place for negativity on a team page.

4.   Schedule Your Time. Time blocking is essential to leadership – and to your business. Consistency is the key to leadership. Simply show up, no matter what.

You should have at LEAST twenty minutes a day to work on your personal business and twenty minutes a day to work on your team. Consider the following:

Monday: Contact all new consultants who have joined in the last week, or even the last few months. Send out new consultant letters/email/packets.

Tuesday: Training. Share some kind of training. Remember, it doesn't have to be yours!

Wednesday: Celebrate earners, promotions, new consultant goals/programs, company incentives – whatever it may be.

Thursday: connect with your up and coming leaders. Doesn't mean they have to have a title. Some of my best leaders don't have a title yet to prove it. CONNECT.

Friday: Plan of action. Give them something to DO and the steps to do it. "Let's all make hostess packets." "Let's all connect with five past hostesses this weekend."

See? It doesn't have to be hard. We're not all born leaders. I know I wasn't. I had to work hard at figuring all this out – And work harder once I realized that I was making it too complicated. It's not. So don't make it be!

Melissa Fietsam
Independent Executive Director, Thirty-One Gifts
buymybags.com

Meredith Hicks

Tech and Team Building

Communication with your team is such an imperative part of building a successful business. I wanted my team to have access to important documents and videos at a moment's notice. I chose to utilize Google Drive in order to create a cloud-based training system that is for information sharing across all levels of my team. It's highly duplicable and new members can be plugged in easily.

We had initial success; however, one hiccup occurred with some team members needing additional training. I created a road map for my team outlining a way forward and a step-by-step user guide for the tool. My team members come from all walks of life and all levels of technical skills. Some join as Preferred Customers so they don't need much training beyond how to order their own products from the website. Others join to build their own teams.

I used the PDF format for my document, since it's easy to update and it helps them create duplication. Being accessible in real-time lets my team members decide when and how much they want to learn. They can plug their own downline into the PDF, and then be available afterwards for questions that may arise. The document is available right on the Google Drive, as well as our team's Facebook Group. Working together, we all succeed!

Resources used by my team:

- ***Google Drive.*** *A file storage and synchronization service developed by Google. Allows users to store files in the cloud, synchronize files across devices, and share files.*

- ***Adobe PDF.*** *View, create, manipulate, print and manage files in Portable Document Format (PDF).*

- ***CinchShare.*** *Web-based program that allows users to schedule posts to Personal Profiles, Business Pages, and Groups.*

- ***Facebook Live Broadcasts (Team Trainings).*** *Held in the teams Facebook Group.*

- ***Facebook Messenger Group Chat.***

- ***OBS Studio.*** *Free and open source software suite for recording and live streaming. OBS provides real-time source and device capture, scene composition, encoding, recording and broadcasting.*

- ***IAG.me.*** *Locate the stream key to go live almost anywhere on your Facebook*

- ***Zoom Meeting.*** *This simple to use platform is for video conferencing. Participants screen share and have face to face video chat. Problem solving is simplified by using video.*

- ***Mobizen (Android).*** *Allows the user to screen record a mobile device or even control it using the computer. This is great when screen sharing with the team and demonstrating how to use an app or page on a mobile device.*

- ***Movavi Screen Record Suite.*** *Records the PC screen for making training videos. Utilizing the Suite allows the user to also edit the videos and add components like voiceover, captions etc.*

- ***Social Jukebox.*** *Eliminate the need to continually schedule your tweets, and manage your content. It's all right at your fingertips. Once you turn on your jukebox, it posts for you, automatically. Load a jukebox with content, figure out how often you'd like it to tweet, and then turn it on.*

Meredith Hicks
Independent JR Watkins Consultant
ournaturalclan.ca/shop

Sarah Fisher Durst

Who is a former elementary school teacher and drug addict, and now a successful entrepreneur? Me!! Sarah Fisher Durst! I taught elementary school for eleven years, abused drugs for countless years, and eventually things fell apart.

It took some time but I cleaned up my life and found myself in a different city living with an amazing man. We had children. And then he dropped a bomb on me and asked me to return to teaching once both our kids were in school — talk about panic!!! I didn't know what to do. I knew nothing about working online. I had no idea the what, the how, the who, the company, the products. I didn't know anything other than I didn't want to go back to teaching.

As a result, I started my first network marketing business in May 2014, a full year before my son was scheduled to start school, and had high hopes that I wouldn't have to return to work as a teacher.

Because I didn't know what I didn't know, I proceeded to spend hours upon hours posting Craigslist ads and spamming everyone I knew. I literally went through Facebook and my entire friends list and sent everyone a message with a link and a couple of videos and just a lot of canned sounding words. And guess what? It didn't work. LOL! I didn't make sales and I didn't add business partners and I didn't make any money. In fact, I lost some Facebook friends and had a growing stockpile of autoshipped products.

Now, the thing is I knew that this industry was powerful. I had met people that were having HUGE success. I knew that people were making money. I knew that regular people, just like me, were winning — and that there was nothing different or special about them other than they seemed to have cracked some magical code. I later found out that this code is nothing more than meeting new people and sharing my products and opportunity with them and asking them to join. MEET — SHARE — ASK!

I knew that my next steps toward financial success were as simple as speaking with more people. With Facebook, the world was wide open. Because of my earlier failure with Facebook and spamming people I realized that I needed to do something different. I couldn't copy and paste the same images that I saw other people using. I couldn't promote my business all the time.

What I could do was share me – share my strengths and weaknesses, my quirks and my humour. I let people in and they responded with positivity. I also realized that I could grow my business with Facebook, BUT I would need to grow my network too. My 300 friends weren't going to get me to the top of any company. I made a conscious decision to be a Facebook marketer and then took steps to build my friends and followers list.

My profile is for business and I make my posts public. I am not worried about posting about my kids, etc. because I choose everything that I put on my timeline with care. If I don't want people to know something or see something, then I just don't post it. Fancy that – not posting everything in your life, especially the things that don't need public opinion.

It has taken me almost two years to get to a point in my business where I am confident posting and sharing about myself and my business. I don't post a lot about my business and I try to make my posts more original than the image my company sends out. I don't want to be in someone's timeline sharing the same image that other people have already shared. I want to be unique. I want to be authentic. I want to be real. I know it is working because I have grown my team with Facebook.

This brings me to the point of this little essay: Facebook marketing can be very powerful. However, not all Facebook marketing is equal. In order to get the most value on Facebook you need to take a good look at your timeline and what you are posting. You need to DECIDE what your goal with Facebook is. Do you want to share with a few friends or do you want to build an empire? If you choose to build an empire, then you need to suck it up and take steps to grow your network in an open manner. It is important to note here that not all "friends" are equal. Discovering who your ideal customer is will help your business immensely. If your network is made up of random people, you will struggle to grow your business. However, if your network is filled with your ideal customers and business partners, you will experience more success.

Facebook is SOCIAL media, so you need to be social. Be active on your timeline with posts that are engaging. Ask questions or take surveys. Post in groups, comment on other people's posts, support, empower, encourage, make referrals, and be open to being vulnerable. Consistency is KEY in terms of what and how frequently you are posting.

The most important thing to remember about Facebook is that it is a TOOL for you to use to grow your network. As you grow your network you will connect on a deeper level using Facebook Messenger. This is where the real magic happens. You need to connect with people (outside of your posts) in a meaningful and authentic manner.

Ask people questions, learn about their lives, what are they missing, what are they looking for – identify their problem and be the solution. You have to BUILD relationships with people before they are going to join your business. That is why you share about yourself with your posts – so people can learn to know, like and trust you. Then you connect deeper through private messages and make magic!

Serious success can be achieved through Facebook marketing. It will take time. You can't expect to make one post and see the $$$$$ rolling in. You need to grow your network with your ideal customers. You need to nurture your network and offer valuable content to them. Don't be negative or post things on Facebook that really should be private. If your business is on Facebook, then treat it like a business. And lastly, think about this – over 80 percent of women in the US *that earn over $100,000 do it from a home-based business! Are you next?*

Sarah Fisher Durst
Whiz-Bang Lady Boss
sarahfisherdurst.com

Shelly Keene

How to Attract New Leads on Social Media by Not Being THAT Person

Social media has become THE way to do business. I will admit that I prefer person-to-person contact. I enjoy the experience of getting to know my customers and being able to offer them a more personal experience.

That being said, I also need to adjust my business to attract new leads without being spammy! That's right — I said it! The following are some Do's and Don'ts of social media that will help you get new leads as well as attract more people to your business in the future.

DO:

- *Post a question like, "Help me choose from my head shots for my business." This will attract more people to your business and have them feel like their opinions matter.*

- *Place an occasional ad from your Business Page. This will attract new likes and comments and it doesn't need to be pricey!*

- *You must have lifestyle posts; this lets people know that you are human and when it all comes down to it, people like and need human contact.*

- *Do a giveaway! It doesn't have to be a "Like and Share" or a "place an order and I'll give you . . . ." It can be as simple as "What tea should I have today"? or "It's my birthday and I would like to give to you!"*

- *Facebook Parties seem to be the way of the future. If your business allows, make sure you get commitment from your guests 1 ½ -2 weeks in advance so you are able to send out a catalog and some samples. This keeps your guests engaged as they get to sample the product and have a hard copy catalog to shop from!*

- *As a leader, you need to remember those that helped you get there; you did not do it on your own. Make sure you are engaged with your team and you are able to offer the support that they need.*

The more you engage your community, the more they will trust you and want to do business with you. Worst case scenario — they don't place an order BUT they recommend you to others!
If you are doing the following please stop:

- *Don't create a group on Facebook and add everyone you know; this is a real turn off. ASK FIRST! Respect the fact that they may not want to join now but maybe in the future.*

- *Don't constantly post "Book a party with me," or "Join my team," or "Place an order," etc. People will start to think that all you want them around for is their orders and parties.*

- *When sharing your business opportunity publicly or on Social Media, don't withhold information. Be honest. You don't want people to wonder what it is you actually do! This happens all too often when direct sellers make "claims" that you can earn X amount of dollars by staying home and working the hours you want. This is misleading. Your earning potential depends on how much work you put into your business. People need to know that!*

There is a statement in social media and direct sales and that is the "90-10 rule." If you have not yet heard this, then it means post 90 percent lifestyle, 10 percent sales-y. Use it. It actually works!

Shelly Keene
Steeped Tea Inc. / Independent Consultant - Group Director
mysteepedtea.com/teawithshelly

Sue Valade

I thought I'd share my new way to communicate and generate excitement, which I have seen spark incentive and motivation within my TEAm!

I am a Group Leader with Steeped Tea and I have just started using Facebook Live! What a huge difference in the responses from my team!

I also find that the "live" option for posting something generates much more excitement, because they can hear it in my voice and see it on my face! This is a tremendous feature that I will be using all the time!

Sue Valade

Steeped Tea Inc. / Independent Consultant - Group Leader

Steeped Tea Canada

mysteepedtea.com/suevalade

In Closing . . .

Final Thoughts

In the beginning of this book I told you the story about my very first upline leader, Lucy Brown, and my journey to connecting with her and the inspiration that she gave me.

I recently had the opportunity to reconnect with Lucy and I told her that I had mentioned her in this book. I sent her the introduction to read in advance and she had this to say in response:

It is very heartwarming to hear after so many years that you have made a difference in someone's life. You joined at a time when I was still trying to build a business that was always changing, depending on my own accomplishments as a leader, which were usually a "first" in a young company that had turned to direct sales.

I was still running my business as a "mom" trying to take care of all those team members under me by just getting in my car and heading to them to teach hands-on everything I knew for success. When you joined, you made my business even more successful by introducing social media. It was a little frightening to me because I knew very little about reaching out with this new way of sharing our product. It became exciting, though, to watch our team grow across the entire United States.

I don't know that I really shared with many people how rewarding to my self-esteem direct sales was for a 28-year-old divorced woman with four children. I believe that my love of the products and my belief in what we were sharing drove me to succeed and accomplish things that I never dreamed I could.

As you continue on your own leadership journey, I hope that you will experience, like Lucy, the richness that every connection brings to your life, your business, and your legacy. Empowering others to live out their dreams is something that always rewards you as a leader—as well as your team members! I always say that social media is about connecting with people, not collecting people. The same is true for growing and supporting your team! Here's to the many connections you will make on your leadership journey, made even more successful through the use of technology!

Acknowledgements

Debbie Ternes, CFLC, has been my life and business coach since just after I finished my first book, *Social Media for Direct Selling Representatives* in late 2015. During the year that followed, she gently guided me in taking my personal business to heights I had never seen before. Her intuitive and loving manner of keeping me accountable for the things I say I want to do resulted in my nearly doubling my income in 2016. She taught me how to trust more and prioritize and how to acknowledge my feelings and act anyway. I look forward to continuing to work with her for a very long time!

When somebody who has built a professional speaking business decides to venture out and produce a book filled with their expertise and guidance, many are frustrated by the process of finding a publisher or trusting a self publishing agency. In 2015 my long time friend and colleague, Ruth Schwartz, offered to be my book midwife, and my business was changed forever. Self-publishing a book is a daunting task, but Ruth is an expert at making sure all of the moving parts work like a well-oiled machine. She has empowered me to think bigger, and get my message out to more people through the written word. This book and the first one would not exist or found the success they have without Ruth. She truly is THE Wonderlady!

Given the wild ride that I have experienced in the past year, I cannot forget to acknowledge my husband Greg and my children, Fallon, Alia and Terry. More success came with more time spent away from home, and my family did not skip a beat! Greg and I have become partners and the kids have seen once again what it's like for someone to relentlessly pursue their goals while staying true to their values. I could not ask for more!

Lastly, I would like to thank those who supported me in my early years of leadership, including my former director, Lucy Brown, and the company founders Lori Whiting and Patti Gardner who had faith in me and my unconventional road to success. I also must acknowledge the role that the ELITE Leadership® Certification Course from the DSWA had on the development of my leadership skills. Although I am no longer involved with the DSWA, the impact it had on my business, and friendships that developed among the first to graduate has been long lasting.

Contributors

Heartfelt gratitude to my generous social media connections who contributed their thoughts and ideas to this publication (listed alphabetically by first name):

- Connie Ignacio
- Imee Birkett
- Jennifer Harmon
- Jennifer Johnson
- Jennifer Quisenberry
- Kim Chapman
- Laurie Wright
- Lisa Muth
- Melissa Fietsam
- Meredith Hicks
- Sarah Fisher Durst
- Shelly Keene
- Sue Valade

About the Author

Nothing replaces connecting with people in person or by phone, and as an experienced and active sales leader, Karen has **walked the walk** as she sold, booked, and supported a team offline, while expanding her reach and service online and through the media. She enjoys teaching others to discover exactly where, when, and how to spend their precious time to establish a presence, while remaining true to their principles and personal business. She brings powerful messages of ethics, effectiveness and efficiency in social media and Internet marketing to direct sales and other home-based entrepreneur audiences. Her programs are high content and filled with actionable strategies that can be implemented immediately.

For companies who want to grow their bottom line, or for distributors and leaders who want to have more of an impact,

Karen offers dynamic programs based on years of hands-on experience. She understands that you have a choice when it comes to learning about social media or bringing someone in to speak at your events. What makes her different?

- **Her experience** — As a pioneer in using technology in the industry, Karen spent twelve years in the field. She has seen and done it all, both online and in a traditional in-home party business, leading a large organization. She speaks the language of direct sales, having taken the company to the Internet across the US and rising through the ranks from Consultant to top Director to Corporate Trainer, leaving that company to **operate independently** as a social media speaker starting in 2009. If you are looking for a presenter who is not enrolled in or employed by any one direct selling company, Karen would love to work with you.

- **Her content**. It's simple, easy to implement and profit-producing, yet based on years of practical experience and continued study of social media and Internet marketing topics. Karen can help your representatives **shorten their learning curves** through distilling just what's important to them in their situation, target demographic and product line, so that they can get down to business and get results. Her content is customized with real examples that model appropriate and effective tactics.

- **Her delivery**. Karen is fun and friendly, and her enthusiasm and passion for the industry inspires people to make the most of their social media time. As someone who tends to bridge many age ranges, audiences **find her relatable** and they take her training to heart because she "gets" them and their lifestyle as a home-based business owner. People trust that Karen has their interests at heart and are therefore eager to implement what she teaches them. There's no hype, just practical content based on someone who is a lot like them.

- **Her professionalism**. As a paid professional speaker, Karen prides herself in exceeding her clients' expectations through timely and positive communication, flexibility and excellence on stage and behind the scenes. She carefully works with meeting planners to deliver the very best and most powerful program that will lead to measurable change. As a Professional Member of the National Speakers Association since 2011, Karen holds herself to a **high standard of enterprise, eloquence, expertise and ethics**. She feels it is an honor to do what she does and she takes it very seriously.

- **Her presence**. Karen becomes part of your event—**approachable and accessible**. She will not simply arrive, "perform," sell product, and leave. She enjoys being at your event and getting to know your representatives and corporate team. She truly loves and supports all those involved in the industry and it shows! This builds trust and a sense of comfort from your audience when she asks them to look at technology in new and sometimes unfamiliar ways.

- **Her impact**. Karen empowers home-based entrepreneurs to focus, to be more efficient and to get results fast using strategies and **tactics they can immediately implement** following—or sometimes during—your event. Her emphasis is on inspiring direct sellers to truly connect with people online and then to continue relationship-building in a combination of both new and traditional methods—not simply collecting people to sell to.

Taking her own direct selling business to the very highest level of the compensation plan in less than seven years was just the start. As the Director of Consultant Development for the company, Karen created training programs for the entire field of representatives for five years before founding her company, My Business Presence. She has **practical experience in the field,** giving her a unique ability to convey her message authentically—**She has been there!**

As a fierce advocate for entrepreneurs and the direct selling industry, Karen has been honored with two Direct Selling Women's Alliance awards—the DSWA Spirit Award in 2008 and the DSWA Ambassador of the Year award in 2010. Now operating independently, she is dedicated to helping all entrepreneurs and independent direct sales representatives **uplift the reputation of the industry** as they learn **smart and ethical** Internet marketing strategies.

Karen has been featured in Belinda Ellsworth's *Step Into Success* magazine, as well as *The Home Business Connection, The Network Marketing Magazine,* and *Party Plan Magazine* publications. She was also featured in *Top Sellers Tell,* a book highlighting successful home-based entrepreneurs. In addition to her first book, *Social Media for Direct Selling Representatives* and this book, *Social Media for Direct Selling Leaders,* she is a co-author of the sales guidebook, *Direct Selling Power,* as well as a general business guidebook, *Incredible Business.* She is a contributing author in *Behind Her Brand: Direct Selling Edition* by various direct sales experts, and *Be A Network Marketing Leader* by Mary Christensen. Karen lives with her husband Greg who along with Karen is raising their three children in beautiful Sonoma County, California.

Connect with Karen Clark
My Business Presence

Office Phone: 707-939-5709
Mobile Phone: 707-486-1927
Email: karen@mybusinesspresence.com
Mailing Address: PO Box 1264 Rohnert Park CA 94927
General Website: mybusinesspresence.com
Book Website: socialmediafordirectselling.com

Social Media Sites:
Facebook: facebook.com/mybusinesspresence
LinkedIn: linkedin.com/in/karenmarieclark
Twitter: twitter.com/mybizpresence
Instagram: instagram.com/karenmclark
Pinterest: pinterest.com/karenmclark
YouTube: youtube.com/mybusinesspresence

Use This Book
as a Training Tool

Social Media for Direct Selling Leaders as well as the first in the series, *Social Media for Direct Selling Representatives*, are available in bulk at a discount to companies and leaders, or for drop-shipping as gifts for your team members. Please contact us for pricing.

Connections Press
PO Box 1264
Rohnert Park CA 94928

(707) 939-5709
info@connectionspress.com

49826444R00131

Made in the USA
San Bernardino, CA
05 June 2017